PENGUIN BOOKS

WALKING WITH THE COMRADES

© Sanjay Kak

ARUNDHATI ROY is the author of *The God of Small Things*, which won the prestigious Man Booker Prize in 1997. Since then she has produced numerous works of political commentary and investigative journalism including *An Ordinary Person's Guide to Empire* and *Field Notes on Democracy*. Roy is the recipient of the 2002 Lannan Foundation Cultural Freedom Prize. She lives in New Delhi.

Walking with the Comrades

ARUNDHATI ROY

PENGUIN BOOKS

PENGUIN BOOKS

Published by the Penguin Group

Penguin Group (USA) Inc., 375 Hudson Street, New York, New York 10014, U.S.A.

Penguin Group (Canada), 90 Eglinton Avenue East, Suite 700, Toronto,
Ontario, Canada M4P 2Y3 (a division of Pearson Penguin Canada Inc.)

Penguin Books Ltd, 80 Strand, London WC2R 0RL, England

Penguin Ireland, 25 St Stephen's Green, Dublin 2, Ireland
(a division of Penguin Books Ltd)

Penguin Group (Australia), 250 Camberwell Road, Camberwell,
Victoria 3124, Australia (a division of Pearson Australia Group Pty Ltd)

Penguin Books India Pvt Ltd, 11 Community Centre,
Panchsheel Park, New Delhi – 110 017, India

Penguin Group (NZ), 67 Apollo Drive, Rosedale, Auckland 0632,
New Zealand (a division of Pearson New Zealand Ltd)

Penguin Books (South Africa) (Pty) Ltd, 24 Sturdee Avenue,
Rosebank, Johannesburg 2196, South Africa

Penguin Books Ltd, Registered Offices:
80 Strand, London WC2R 0RL, England

First published in India by Hamish Hamilton, a member of Penguin Books India 2011
Published in Penguin Books (USA) 2012

1   3   5   7   9   10   8   6   4   2

These essays have previously appeared in *Outlook*

Photographs by Sanjay Kak and Arundhati Roy

ISBN 978-0-14-312059-9
CIP data available

Printed in the United States of America
Designed by Bena Sareen

CONTENTS

Your blood asks, how were the wealthy
And the law interwoven? With what
sulfurous iron fabric? How did the
poor keep falling into the tribunals?
—PABLO NERUDA, *The Judges*

The President Took the Salute

The Minister says that for India's sake, people should leave their villages and move to the cities. He's a Harvard man. He wants speed. And numbers. Five hundred million migrants, he thinks, would make a good business model.

Not everybody likes the idea of their cities filling up with the poor. A judge in Mumbai called slum dwellers pickpockets of urban land. Another said, while ordering the bulldozing of unauthorized colonies, that people who couldn't afford it shouldn't live in cities.

When those who had been evicted went back to where they came from, they found their villages had disappeared under great dams and quarries. Their homes were occupied by hunger, and policemen. The forests were filling up with armed guerrillas. War had migrated too. From the edges of India, in Kashmir, Manipur, Nagaland, to its heart. So the people returned to the crowded city streets and pavements. They crammed into hovels on dusty construction sites, wondering which corner of this huge country was meant for them.

The Minister said that migrants to cities were mostly criminals and 'carried a kind of behaviour which is unacceptable to modern cities'. The middle class admired him for his forthrightness, for having the courage to call a spade a spade. The Minister said he would set up more police stations, recruit more policemen and put more police vehicles on the road to improve law and order.

To make Delhi a world-class city for the 2010 Commonwealth Games, laws were passed that made the poor vanish, like laundry stains. Street vendors disappeared, rickshaw pullers lost their licences, small shops and businesses were shut down. Beggars were rounded up, tried by mobile magistrates in mobile courts and dropped outside the city limits. The slums that remained were screened off, with vinyl billboards that said DELHIciously Yours.

New kinds of policemen patrolled the streets, better armed, better dressed and trained not to scratch their privates in public, no matter how grave the provocation. There were cameras everywhere, recording everything.

~

Two young criminals carrying a kind of behaviour which was unacceptable to modern cities escaped the police dragnet, and approached a woman sandwiched between her sunglasses and the leather seats of her shiny car at a traffic crossing. Shamelessly they demanded money. The woman was rich and kind. The criminals' heads were no higher than her car window. Their names were Rukmini and Kamli. Or maybe Mehrunissa and Shahbano. (Who cares?) The woman gave them money and some motherly advice. Ten rupees to Kamli (or Shahbano). 'Share it,' she told them, and sped away when the lights changed.

Rukmini and Kamli (or Mehrunissa and Shahbano) tore into each other like gladiators, like lifers in a prison yard. Each sleek car that flashed past them, and almost crushed them, carried the reflection of their battle, their fight to the finish, on its shining door.

Eventually both girls disappeared without a trace, like thousands of children do in Delhi.

The Games were a success.

~

Two months later, on the sixty-second anniversary of India becoming a Republic, the armed forces showcased their new weapons at the Republic Day parade. Russian multi-barrel rocket launchers, combat aircraft, light helicopters and underwater weapons for the navy. The new T-90 battle tank was called Bhishma. (The older one was Arjun.) Varunastra was the name of the latest heavyweight torpedo, and Mareech was a decoy system to seduce incoming torpedoes. (Hanuman and Vajra are the names painted on the armoured vehicles that patrol Kashmir's frozen streets.) That the names were drawn from Hindu epics was just a coincidence. If India is a Hindu nation, it's only an accident.

Dare Devils from the Army's Corps of Signals rode motorcycles in a rocket formation. Then they formed a cluster of flying birds and finally a human pyramid.

Overhead Sukhoi fighter jets made a trishul, a trident in the sky. Each jet cost more than a billion rupees. Four billion then, for Shiva's Trident.

The thrilled crowd turned its face up to the weak, winter sun and applauded. High in the sky, the winking silver sides of the jets carried the reflection of Rukmini's and Kamli's (or Mehrunissa's and Shahbano's) fight to the death.

The army band played the national anthem. The President drew the pallu of her sari over her head and took the salute.

February 2011

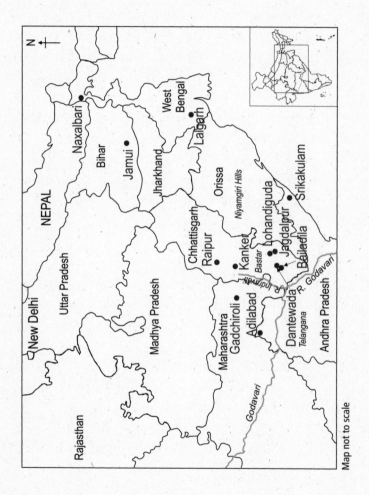

Map not to scale

Walking with the Comrades

Mr Chidambaram's War

The low, flat-topped hills of south Orissa have been home to the Dongria Kondh long before there was a country called India or a state called Orissa. The hills watched over the Kondh. The Kondh watched over the hills and worshipped them as living deities. Now these hills have been sold for the bauxite they contain. For the Kondh it's as though god has been sold. They ask how much god would go for if the god were Ram or Allah or Jesus Christ.

Perhaps the Kondh are supposed to

be grateful that their Niyamgiri hill, home to their Niyam Raja, God of Universal Law, has been sold to a company with a name like Vedanta (the branch of Hindu philosophy that teaches the Ultimate Nature of Knowledge). It's one of the biggest mining corporations in the world and is owned by Anil Agarwal, the Indian billionaire who lives in London in a mansion that once belonged to the Shah of Iran. Vedanta is only one of the many multinational corporations closing in on Orissa.[1]

If the flat-topped hills are destroyed, the forests that clothe them will be destroyed too. So will the rivers and streams that flow out of them and irrigate the plains below. So will the Dongria Kondh. So will the hundreds of thousands of tribal people who live in the forested heart of India, whose homeland is similarly under attack.

In our smoky, crowded cities, some people say, 'So what? Someone has to pay the price of progress.' Some even say, 'Let's face it, these are people whose time has come. Look at any developed country, Europe, the United States, Australia—they all have a "past".' Indeed they do. So why shouldn't 'we'?

In keeping with this line of thought, the government has announced Operation Green Hunt, a war purportedly against the 'Maoist' rebels headquartered in the jungles of central India. Of course, the Maoists are by no means the only ones rebelling. People are engaged in a whole spectrum of struggles all over the country—the landless, the homeless, Dalits, workers, peasants, weavers. They're pitted against a juggernaut of injustices, including policies that allow a wholesale corporate takeover of people's land and resources. However, it is the Maoists the government has singled out as being the biggest threat.

A few years ago, when things were nowhere near as bad as they are now, the prime minister described the Maoists as 'the single biggest internal security challenge ever faced by our country'.[2] This will probably go down as the most popular and often-repeated thing he ever said. For some reason, the comment he made in January 2009, at a meeting of state chief ministers, when he described the Maoists' army as one of 'modest proportions' doesn't seem to have had the same raw appeal.[3] He revealed his government's real concern on 9 June 2009, when he told Parliament: 'if Left Wing extremism continues to flourish in important parts of our country which have tremendous natural resources of minerals and other precious things, that will certainly affect the climate for investment'.[4]

Who are the Maoists? They are members of the banned Communist Party of India (Maoist)—CPI (Maoist)—one of the several descendants of the Communist Party of India (Marxist-Leninist), which led

BAUXITE MINES, DAMANJODI, ORISSA, 2005

If the flat-topped hills are destroyed, the forests that clothe them will be destroyed too. So will the rivers and streams that flow out of them and irrigate the plains below. So will the Dongria Kondh. So will the hundreds of thousands of tribal people who live in the forested heart of India, and whose homeland is similarly under attack.

NIYAMGIRI, ORISSA, 2010
The hills watched over the
Kondh. The Kondh watched over
the hills and worshipped them
as living deities.

the 1969 Naxalite uprising in West Bengal. The Maoists believe that the innate, structural inequality of Indian society can only be redressed by the violent overthrow of the Indian State. In its earlier avatars as the Maoist Communist Centre (MCC) in Jharkhand and Bihar, and the People's War Group (PWG) in Andhra Pradesh, the Maoists had tremendous popular support. (When the ban on them was briefly lifted in 2004, more than a million people attended their rally in Warangal, Andhra Pradesh.)

But eventually their intercession in Andhra Pradesh ended badly. They left a violent legacy that turned some of their staunchest supporters into harsh critics. After a paroxysm of killing and counter-killing by the Andhra police as well as the rebels, the PWG was decimated. Those who managed to survive fled Andhra Pradesh into neighbouring Chhattisgarh. There, deep in the heart of the forest, they joined colleagues who had already been working there for decades.

Not many 'outsiders' have any first-hand experience of the real nature of the Maoist movement in the forest. A recent interview with one of its top leaders, Comrade Ganapathy, didn't do much to change the minds of those who view the Maoists as a party with an unforgiving, totalitarian vision, which countenances no dissent whatsoever.[5] Comrade Ganapathy said nothing that would persuade people that were the Maoists ever to come to power, they would be equipped to properly address the almost insane diversity of India's caste-ridden society. His casual approval of the Liberation Tigers of Tamil Eelam (LTTE) of Sri Lanka was enough to send a shiver down even the most sympathetic of spines, not just because of the brutal ways in which the LTTE chose to wage its war, but also because of the cataclysmic tragedy that has befallen the Tamil people of Sri Lanka, whom it claimed to represent, and for whom it surely must take some responsibility.

Right now in central India, the Maoists' guerrilla army is made up almost entirely of desperately poor tribal people living in conditions of such chronic hunger that it verges on famine of the kind we only associate with sub-Saharan Africa. They are people who, even after sixty years of India's so-called Independence, have not had access to education, health care or legal redress. They are people who have been mercilessly exploited for decades, consistently cheated by small businessmen and moneylenders, the women raped as a matter of right by police and forest department personnel. Their journey back to a semblance of dignity is due in large part to the Maoist cadre who have lived and worked and fought by their side for decades.

If the tribals have taken up arms, they have done so because a government that has given them nothing but violence and neglect now wants to snatch away the last thing they have—their land. Clearly, they do not believe the government when it says it only wants to 'develop' their region. Clearly, they do not believe that the roads as wide and flat as aircraft runways that are being built through their forests in Dantewada by the National Mineral Development Corporation are being built for them to walk their children to school. They believe that

if they do not fight for their land, they will be annihilated. That is why they have taken up arms.

Even if the ideologues of the Maoist movement are fighting to eventually overthrow the Indian State, right now even they know that their ragged, malnutritioned army, the bulk of whose soldiers have never seen a train or a bus or even a small town, is fighting only for survival.

In 2008 an expert group appointed by the Planning Commission submitted a report called *Development Challenges in Extremist Affected Areas*. It said, 'the Naxalite (Maoist) movement has to be recognised as a political movement with a strong base among the landless and poor peasantry and adivasis. Its emergence and growth need to be contextualised in the social conditions and experience of people who form a part of it. The huge gap between state policy and performance is a feature of these conditions. Though its professed long-term

ideology is capturing state power by force, in its day-to-day manifestation, it is to be looked upon as basically a fight for social justice, equality, protection, security and local development.'[6] A very far cry from the 'single biggest internal security challenge'.

Since the Maoist rebellion is the flavour of the week, everybody, from the sleekest fat cat to the most cynical editor of the most sold-out newspaper in this country, seems to be suddenly ready to concede that it is decades of accumulated injustice that lies at the root of the problem. But instead of addressing that problem, which

Thirteen tonnes of stone and rock yield one tonne of bauxite. The 'Red Mud' in these stilling ponds is the toxic residue produced by the refining process in which bauxite is turned into aluminium.

would mean putting the brakes on this twenty-first-century gold rush, they are trying to head the debate off in a completely different direction, with a noisy outburst of pious outrage about Maoist 'terrorism'. But they're only speaking to themselves.

The people who have taken to arms are not spending their time watching (or performing for) TV, or reading the papers, or conducting SMS polls for the Moral Science question of the day: Is Violence Good or Bad? SMS your reply to... They're out there. They're fighting. They believe they have the right to defend their homes and their land. They believe that they deserve justice.

In order to keep its better-off citizens absolutely safe, the government has declared war on these dangerous people. A war which, it tells us, may take between three and five years to win. There's no whisper about 'talks' or 'negotiations'. Odd, isn't it, that even after the Mumbai attacks of 26/11 the government was prepared to talk with Pakistan? It's prepared to talk to China. But when it comes to waging war against the poor, it's playing hard-ball.

It's not enough that Special Police—with totemic names like Greyhounds, Cobras and Scorpions—are scouring the forests with a licence to kill. It's not enough that the Central Reserve Police Force (CRPF), the Border Security Force (BSF) and the notorious

Naga Battalion have already wreaked havoc and committed unconscionable atrocities in remote forest villages. It's not enough that the government supports and arms the Salwa Judum, the 'people's militia' that has killed and raped and burned its way through the forests of Dantewada, leaving 50,000 people in roadside police camps and the rest of the population in the area (about 300,000 people) homeless, or on the run. Now the government is going to deploy the Indo-Tibetan Border Police and tens of thousands of paramilitary troops. According to one report it plans to set up a brigade headquarters in Bilaspur (which will displace nine villages) and an air base in Rajnandgaon (which will displace seven).[7] Obviously, these decisions were taken a while ago. Surveys have been done, sites chosen. Interesting. War has been in the offing for a while. And now the helicopters of the Indian Air Force have been given the right to fire in 'self-defence', the very right that the government denies its poorest citizens.

Fire at whom? How in god's name will the security forces be able to distinguish a Maoist from an ordinary person who is running terrified through the jungle? Will adivasis carrying the bows and arrows they have carried for centuries now count as Maoists too? Are non-combatant Maoist sympathizers valid targets? When I was in Dantewada, the superintendent of police showed me pictures of nineteen 'Maoists' whom 'his boys' had killed. I asked him how I was supposed to tell they were Maoists. He said, 'See ma'am, they have malaria medicines, Dettol bottles, all these things from outside.'

What kind of war is Operation Green Hunt going to be? Will we ever know? Not much news comes out of the forests. Lalgarh in West Bengal has been cordoned off. Those who try to go in are being beaten and arrested. And called Maoists of course. In Dantewada, the Vanvasi Chetana Ashram, a Gandhian ashram run by Himanshu Kumar, was bulldozed in a few hours. It was the last neutral outpost before the war zone begins, a place where journalists, activists, researchers and fact-finding teams could stay while they worked in the area.

Meanwhile, the Indian establishment has unleashed its most potent weapon. Almost overnight, our embedded media has substituted its steady supply of planted, unsubstantiated, hysterical stories about 'Islamist Terrorism' with planted, unsubstantiated, hysterical stories about 'Red Terrorism'. In the midst of this racket, at Ground Zero, the cordon of silence is being inexorably tightened. The 'Sri Lanka Solution' could very well be on the cards. Could this be why the Indian government blocked a European move in the UN asking for an international probe into war crimes committed by the government of Sri Lanka in its recent offensive against the Tamil Tigers?[8]

The first move in that direction is the concerted campaign that has been orchestrated to shoehorn the myriad forms of resistance taking place in this country into a simple George Bush binary: If you are not with us, you are with the Maoists. The deliberate exaggeration of the Maoist 'threat' helps the State to justify militarization. (And surely does no harm to the Maoists. Which political party would be unhappy to be singled out for such attention?) While all the oxygen is being used up by this new doppelganger of the War on Terror, the State will use the opportunity to mop up the hundreds of other resistance movements in the sweep of its military operation, calling them all Maoist sympathizers.

I use the future tense, but this process is well under way. The West Bengal government tried to do this in Nandigram and Singur but failed. Right now in Lalgarh, the Pulishi Santrash Birodhi Janasadharaner Committee, or the People's Committee against Police Atrocities—which is a people's movement that is separate from, though sympathetic to, the Maoists—is routinely referred to as an overground wing of the CPI (Maoist). Its leader, Chhatradhar Mahato, now arrested and being held without bail, is always called a 'Maoist leader'. We all know the story of Dr Binayak Sen, a medical doctor and a civil liberties activist, who spent two years in jail on the absolutely facile charge of being a courier for the

IRON-ORE CRUSHING PLANT, KEONJHAR, ORISSA, 2005
While for the adivasis the mountain is still a living deity, the fountainhead of
life and faith, the keystone of the ecological health of the region, for
the corporation, it's just a cheap storage facility. Goods in storage have
to be accessible.

IRON-ORE DUST ON
MANGO LEAVES
There's an MoU on every
mountain, river and forest
glade. We're talking about
social and environmental
engineering on an
unimaginable scale.

Maoists.[9] While the light shines brightly on Operation Green Hunt, in other parts of India, away from the theatre of war, the assault on the rights of the poor, of workers, of the landless, of those whose lands the government wishes to acquire for 'public purpose', will pick up pace. Their suffering will deepen and it will be that much harder for them to get a hearing.

Once the war begins, like all wars, it will develop a momentum, a logic and an economics of its own. It will become a way of life, almost impossible to reverse. The police will be expected to behave like an army, a ruthless killing machine. The paramilitary will be expected to become like the police, a corrupt, bloated administrative force. We've seen it happen in Nagaland, Manipur and Kashmir. The only difference in the 'heartland' will be that it'll become obvious very quickly to the security forces that they're only a little less wretched than the people they're fighting. In time, the divide between the people and the law enforcers will become porous. Guns and ammunition will be bought and sold. (It's already happening.) Whether it's the security forces or the Maoists or non-combatant civilians, the poorest people will die in this Rich People's War. And if anybody believes that this war will leave them unaffected, they should think again. The resources it'll consume will cripple the economy of this country.

Last week, civil liberties groups from all over the country organized a series of meetings in Delhi to discuss what could be done to turn the tide and stop the war. The absence of Dr Balagopal, one of the best-known civil rights activists of Andhra Pradesh, who died two weeks ago, closed around us like a physical pain. He was one of the bravest, wisest political thinkers of our time and left us just when we needed him most. Still, I'm sure he would have been reassured to hear speaker after speaker displaying the vision, the depth, the experience, the wisdom, the political acuity and, above all, the real humanity of the community of activists, academics, lawyers, judges and a range of other people who make up the civil liberties community in India. Their presence in the capital signalled that outside the arc lights of our TV studios and beyond the drumbeat of media hysteria, even among India's middle classes, a humane heart still beats. Small wonder then that these are the people whom the Union home minister recently accused of creating an 'intellectual climate' that was conducive to 'terrorism'. If that charge was meant to frighten people, to cow them down, it had the opposite effect.

The speakers represented a range of opinion from the liberal to the radical Left. Though none of those who spoke would describe themselves as Maoist, few were opposed in principle to the idea that people have a right to defend themselves against State violence. Many were uncomfortable about Maoist violence, about the 'people's courts' that delivered summary justice, about the authoritarianism that was bound to permeate an armed struggle and marginalize those who did not have arms. But even as they expressed their discomfort, they knew that people's courts only existed because India's courts are out of the reach of ordinary people and that the armed struggle that has broken out in the heartland is not the first, but the very last option of a desperate people pushed to the very brink of existence. The speakers were aware of the dangers of trying to extract a simple morality out of individual incidents of heinous violence, in a situation that had already begun to look very much like war. Everybody had graduated long ago from equating the structural violence of the state with the violence of the armed resistance. In fact, retired Justice P.B. Sawant went so far as to thank the Maoists for forcing the establishment of this country to pay attention to the egregious injustice of the system.[10] Hargopal from Andhra Pradesh spoke of his experience as a civil rights activist through the years of the Maoist interlude in his state. He said that in a few days in Gujarat, in 2002, Hindu mobs led by the Bajrang Dal and the Vishwa Hindu Parishad (VHP) killed more people than the Maoists ever had even in their bloodiest days in Andhra Pradesh.[11]

People who had come from the war zones, from Lalgarh, Jharkhand, Chhattisgarh and Orissa, described the repression, the arrests, the torture, the killing, the corruption, and the fact that, in places like Orissa, the police seemed to take orders directly from the officials who worked for the mining companies. People described the dubious, malign role being played by certain NGOs funded by aid agencies wholly devoted to furthering corporate prospects. Again and again they spoke of how in Jharkhand and Chhattisgarh activists as well as ordinary people—anyone who was seen to be a dissenter—were being branded Maoists and imprisoned. They said that this, more than anything else, was pushing people to take up arms and join the Maoists. They asked how a government that professed its inability to resettle even a fraction of the fifty million people who had been displaced by 'development' projects was suddenly able to identify 140,000 hectares of prime land to give to industrialists to set up special economic zones, India's

In Gandhamardhan an old trooper debunks the legendary story about the villagers' 'Gandhian' protest against the mining company Balco. People beat up surveyors, put sugar in a bulldozer tank and pushed a jeep over a cliff, she says.

onshore tax havens for the rich.[12] They asked what brand of justice the Supreme Court was practising when it refused to review the meaning of 'public purpose' in the Land Acquisition Act even when it knew that the government was forcibly acquiring land in the name of 'public purpose' to give to private corporations. They asked why, when the government says that 'the Writ of the State must run', it seems to only mean that police stations must be put in place. Not schools or clinics or housing, or clean water, or a fair price for forest produce, or even being left alone and free from the fear of the police—anything that would make people's lives a little easier. They asked why the 'Writ of the State' could never be taken to mean justice.

There was a time, perhaps ten years ago, when, in meetings like these, people were still debating the model of 'development' that was being thrust on them by the New Economic Policy. Now the rejection of that model is complete. It is absolute. Everyone from the Gandhians to the Maoists agrees on that. The only question now is, what is the most effective way to dismantle it?

An old college friend of a friend, a big noise in the corporate world, had come along for one of the meetings out of morbid curiosity about a world he knew very little about. Even though he had disguised himself in a Fabindia kurta, he couldn't help looking (and smelling) expensive. At one point, he leaned across to me and said, 'Someone should tell them not to bother. They won't win this one. They have no idea what they're up against. With the kind of money that's involved here, these companies can buy ministers and media barons and policy wonks, they can run their own NGOs, their own militias, they can buy whole governments. They'll even buy the Maoists. These good people here should save their breath and find something better to do.'

When people are being brutalized, what 'better' thing is there for them to do than to fight back? It's not as though anyone's offering them a choice, unless it's to commit suicide, like the 180,000 farmers caught in a spiral of debt have done. (Am I the only one who gets the distinct feeling that the Indian establishment and its representatives in the media are far more comfortable with the idea of poor people killing themselves in despair than with the idea of them fighting back?)

For several years, people in Chhattisgarh, Orissa, Jharkhand and West Bengal—some of them Maoists, many not—have managed to hold off the big corporations. The question now is, how will Operation Green Hunt change the nature of their struggle? What exactly are the fighting people up against?

It's true that, historically, mining companies have almost always won their battles against local people.

Of all corporations, leaving aside the ones that make weapons, they probably have the most merciless past. They are cynical, battle-hardened campaigners and when people say, *'Jaan denge par jameen nahin denge'* (We'll give away our lives, but never our land), it probably bounces off them like a light drizzle on a bomb shelter. They've

heard it before, in a thousand different languages, in a hundred different countries.

Right now in India, many of them are still in the first-class arrivals lounge, ordering cocktails, blinking slowly like lazy predators, waiting for the memorandums of understanding (MoUs) they have signed—some as far back as 2005—to materialize into real money. But four years in a first-class lounge is enough to test the patience of even the truly tolerant. There's only that much space they're willing to make for the elaborate, if increasingly empty, rituals of democratic practice: the (rigged) public hearings, the (fake) environmental impact assessments, the (purchased) clearances from various ministries, the long-drawn-out court cases. Even phoney democracy is time-consuming. And time, for industrialists, is money.

So what kind of money are we talking about? In their seminal book *Out of This Earth: East India Adivasis and the*

Aluminium Cartel, Samarendra Das and Felix Padel say that the financial value of the bauxite deposits of Orissa alone is 2.27 trillion dollars (twice India's gross domestic product).[13] That was at 2004 prices. At today's prices it would be about four trillion dollars. A trillion has twelve zeroes.

Of this, officially the government gets a royalty of less than 7 per cent. Quite often, if the mining company is a known and recognized one, chances are that even though the ore is still in the mountain, it will have already been traded on the futures market. So, while for the adivasis the mountain is still a living deity, the

Every year on Independence Day and Republic Day the villagers of Kuchaipadar hoist a black flag in memory of three adivasis the police killed in December 2000 at a protest against Hindalco in Maikanch.

fountainhead of life and faith, the keystone of the ecological health of the region, for the corporation, it's just a cheap storage facility. Goods in storage have to be accessible. From the corporation's point of view, the bauxite will have to come out of the mountain. If it can't be done peacefully, then it will have to be done violently. Such are the pressures and the exigencies of the free market.

That's just the story of the bauxite in Orissa. Expand the four trillion dollars to include the value of the millions of tonnes of high-quality iron ore in Chhattisgarh and Jharkhand and the twenty-eight other precious mineral resources, including uranium, limestone, dolomite, coal, tin, granite, marble, copper, diamond, gold, quartzite, corundum, beryl, alexandrite, silica, fluorite and garnet. Add to that the power plants, the dams, the highways, the steel and cement factories, the aluminium smelters, and all the other infrastructure projects that are part of the hundreds of MoUs (more than ninety in Jharkhand alone) that have been signed. That gives us a rough outline of the scale of the operation and the desperation of the stakeholders.

The forest once known as Dandakaranya, which stretches from West Bengal through Jharkhand, Orissa, Chhattisgarh, and parts of Andhra Pradesh and Maharashtra, is home to millions of India's tribal people.

The media has taken to calling it the Red corridor or the Maoist corridor. It could just as accurately be called the MoUist corridor. The Fifth Schedule of the Constitution provides protection to adivasi people and disallows the alienation of their land. But it doesn't seem to matter at all. It looks as though the clause is there only to make the Constitution look good—a bit of window-dressing, a slash of make-up. Scores of corporations, from relatively unknown ones to the biggest mining companies and steel manufacturers in the world, are in the fray to appropriate adivasi homelands—the Mittals, Jindals, Tata, Essar, Posco, Rio Tinto, BHP Billiton and, of course, Vedanta.

There's an MoU on every mountain, river and forest glade. We're talking about social and environmental engineering on an unimaginable scale. And most of this is secret. It's not in the public domain. Somehow I don't think that the plans that are afoot to destroy one of the world's most pristine forests and ecosystems, as well as the people who live in it, will be discussed at the Climate Change Conference in Copenhagen. Our 24-hour news channels that are so busy hunting for macabre stories of Maoist violence—and making them up when they run out of the real thing—seem to have no interest at all in this side of the story. I wonder why.

Perhaps it's because the development lobby to which they are so much in thrall says the mining industry will ratchet up the rate of GDP growth dramatically, and provide employment to the people it displaces. This does not take into account the catastrophic costs of environmental damage. But even on its own narrow terms, it is simply untrue. Most of the money goes into the bank accounts of the mining corporations. Less than 10 per cent comes to the public exchequer. A very tiny percentage of the displaced people get jobs, and those who do, earn slave wages to do humiliating, back-breaking work. By caving in to this paroxysm of greed, we are bolstering other countries' economies with our ecology.

When the scale of money involved is what it is, the stakeholders are not always easy to identify. Between the CEOs in their private jets and the wretched tribal Special Police Officers in the 'people's' militias—who for a couple of thousand rupees a month fight their own people, rape, kill and burn down whole villages in an effort to clear the ground for mining to begin—there is an entire universe of primary, secondary and tertiary stakeholders. These people don't have to declare their interests, but they're allowed to use their positions and good offices to further them. How will we ever know which political party, which ministers, which MPs, which politicians, which judges, which NGOs, which expert consultants, which police officers, have a direct or indirect stake in the booty? How will we know which newspapers reporting the latest Maoist 'atrocity', which TV channels 'reporting directly from Ground Zero'—or, more accurately, making it a point not to report from Ground Zero or, even more accurately, lying blatantly from Ground Zero—are stakeholders?

What is the provenance of the trillions of dollars (several times more than India's GDP) secretly stashed away by Indian citizens in Swiss bank accounts? Where did the eighty-odd billion rupees spent on the last general elections come from? Where do the hundreds of millions of rupees that political parties and politicians pay the media for the 'high-end', 'low-end' and 'live' pre-election 'coverage packages' that P. Sainath recently wrote about come from?[14] (The next time you see a TV anchor haranguing a numb studio guest, shouting, 'Why don't the Maoists stand for elections? Why don't they come into the mainstream?', do SMS the channel saying, 'Because they can't afford your rates.')

What are we to make of the fact that the Union home minister, P. Chidambaram, the CEO of Operation Green Hunt, has, in his career as a lawyer, represented several mining corporations? What are we to make of the fact that he was a non-executive director of Vedanta—a position from which he resigned the day he became finance minister in 2004? What are we to make of the fact that, when he became finance minister, one of the

A VILLAGE MEETING. KUCHAIPADAR, 2005

Historically, mining companies have almost always won their battles against local people. When people say *'Jaan denge par jameen nahin denge'* (We'll give away our lives, but never our land), it probably bounces off them like a light drizzle on a bomb shelter.

KUCHAIPADAR, 2005
When people are being
brutalized, what 'better' thing
is there for them to do than
to fight back? It's not as
though someone is offering
them a choice.

first clearances he gave for foreign direct investment was to Twinstar Holdings, a Mauritius-based company, to buy shares in Sterlite, a part of the Vedanta group?[15]

What are we to make of the fact that, when activists from Orissa filed a case against Vedanta in the Supreme Court, citing its violations of government guidelines, and pointing out that the Norwegian Pension Fund had withdrawn its investment from the company alleging gross environmental damage and human rights violations committed by the company, Justice Kapadia suggested that Vedanta be substituted with Sterlite? He then blithely announced in an open court that he too had shares in Sterlite. He gave forest clearance to Sterlite to go ahead with the mining despite the fact that the Supreme Court's own expert committee had explicitly said that permission should be denied, and that mining would ruin the forests, water sources, environment and the lives and livelihoods of the thousands of tribals living there. Justice Kapadia gave this clearance without rebutting the report of the Supreme Court's own committee.[16]

What are we to make of the fact that the Salwa Judum, the brutal ground-clearing operation disguised as a 'spontaneous' people's militia in Dantewada, was formally inaugurated in 2005, just days after the MoU with the Tatas was signed? And that the Jungle Warfare College in Kanker was set up just around then?[17]

What are we to make of the fact that on 12 October 2009 the mandatory public hearing for the Tata integrated steel plant in Lohandiguda, Dantewada, was held with a hired audience of fifty tribal people brought into Jagdalpur from two Bastar villages in a convoy of government jeeps? (The public hearing was declared a success and the district collector congratulated the people of Bastar for their cooperation.)

What are we to make of the fact that just around the time the prime minister began to call the Maoists the 'single biggest internal security challenge' (which was a signal that the government was getting ready to go after them) the share prices of many of the mining companies in the region skyrocketed?

The mining companies desperately need this 'war'. It's an old technique. They hope the impact of the violence will drive out the people who have so far managed to resist the attempts that have been made to evict them. Whether this will indeed be the outcome or whether it'll simply swell the ranks of the Maoists remains to be seen.

Reversing this argument, Dr Ashok Mitra, former finance minister of West Bengal, in an article called 'The Phantom Enemy', argues that the 'grisly serial murders' that the Maoists are committing are a classic tactic, learned from guerrilla warfare textbooks. He suggests that they have built and trained a guerrilla army that is now ready to take on the Indian State, and that the Maoist 'rampage' is a deliberate attempt on their part to invite the wrath of a blundering, angry Indian State, which the Maoists hope will commit acts of cruelty that will enrage the adivasis. That rage, Dr Mitra says, is what the Maoists hope can be harvested and transformed into an insurrection.[18]

This, of course, is the charge of 'adventurism' that several currents of the Left have always levelled at the Maoists. It suggests that Maoist ideologues are not above inviting destruction on the very people they claim to represent in order to bring about a revolution that will bring them to power. Ashok Mitra is an old Communist who had a ringside seat during the Naxalite uprising of the '60s and '70s in West Bengal. His views cannot be summarily dismissed. But it's worth keeping in mind that the adivasi people have a long and courageous history of resistance that predates the birth of Maoism. To look upon them as brainless puppets being manipulated by a few middle-class Maoist ideologues is to do them something of a disservice.

Presumably Dr Mitra is talking about the situation in Lalgarh where, up to now, there has been no talk of mineral wealth. (Lest we forget—the current uprising in Lalgarh was sparked off over the chief minister's visit to inaugurate a Jindal Steel factory. And where there's a steel factory, can the iron ore be very far away?) The people's anger has to do with their desperate poverty, and the decades of suffering at the hands of the police and the 'Harmads', the armed militia of the Communist Party of India (Marxist) that has ruled West Bengal for more than thirty years.

Even if, for argument's sake, we don't ask what tens of thousands of police and paramilitary troops are doing in Lalgarh, and we accept the theory of Maoist 'adventurism', it would still be only a very small part of the picture.

The real problem is that the flagship of India's miraculous 'growth' story has run aground. It came at a huge social and environmental cost. And now, as the rivers dry up and forests disappear, as the water table recedes and as people realize what is being done to them, the chickens are coming home to roost. All over the country, there's unrest; there are protests by people refusing to give up their land and their access to resources, refusing to

For years Tula Dei Parabhoi of Sindhbahali refused to move from her home which abutted the boundary walls of Vedanta's refinery in Lanjigarh. The last woman standing is gone now.

believe false promises any more. Suddenly, it's beginning to look as though the 10 per cent growth rate and democracy are mutually incompatible.

To get the bauxite out of the flat-topped hills, to get iron ore out from under the forest floor, to get 85 per cent of India's people off their land and into the cities (which is what Mr Chidambaram says he'd like to see), India has to become a police state. The government has to militarize. To justify that militarization, it needs an enemy. The Maoists are that enemy. They are to corporate fundamentalists what the Muslims are to Hindu fundamentalists. (Is there a fraternity of fundamentalists? Is that why the RSS has expressed open admiration for Mr Chidambaram?)

It would be a grave mistake to imagine that the paramilitary troops, the Rajnandgaon air base, the Bilaspur brigade headquarters, the Unlawful Activities (Prevention) Act, the Chhattisgarh Special Public Security Act and Operation Green Hunt are all being put in place just to flush out a few thousand Maoists from the forests. In all the talk of Operation Green Hunt, whether or not Mr Chidambaram goes ahead and 'presses the button', I detect the kernel of a coming state of emergency. (Here's a maths question: If it takes 600,000 soldiers to hold down the tiny valley of Kashmir, how many will it take to contain the mounting rage of hundreds of millions of people?)

Instead of narco-analysing Kobad Gandhy, the recently arrested Maoist leader, it might be a better idea to *talk* to him.

In the meanwhile, will someone who's going to the Climate Change Conference in Copenhagen later this year please ask the only question worth asking: Can we leave the bauxite in the mountain?

October 2009

Walking with the Comrades

The terse, typewritten note slipped under my door in a sealed envelope confirmed my appointment with 'India's single biggest internal security challenge'. I'd been waiting for months to hear from them.

I had to be at the Ma Danteshwari mandir in Dantewada, Chhattisgarh, at any of four given times on two given days. That was to take care of bad weather, punctures, blockades, transport strikes and sheer bad luck. The note said: 'Writer should have camera, tika and coconut. Meeter will have cap, Hindi *Outlook* magazine and bananas. Password: Namashkar Guruji'.

Namashkar Guruji. I wondered whether the Meeter and Greeter would be expecting a man. And whether I should get myself a moustache.

~

There are many ways to describe Dantewada. It's an oxymoron. It's a border town smack in the heart of India. It's the epicenter of a war. It's an upside-down, inside-out town.

In Dantewada the police wear plain clothes and the rebels wear uniforms. The jail superintendent is in jail. The prisoners are free (three hundred of them escaped from the old town jail two years ago). Women who have been raped are in police custody. The rapists give speeches in the bazaar.

Across the Indravati River, in the area controlled by the Maoists, is the place the police call 'Pakistan'. There the villages are empty, but the forest is full of people. Children who ought to be in school run wild. In the lovely forest villages, the concrete school buildings have either been blown up and lie in a heap or they're full of policemen. The deadly war that's unfolding in the jungle is a war that the Government of India is both proud and shy of. Operation Green Hunt has been proclaimed as well as denied. P. Chidambaram, India's home minister (and CEO of the war), says it does not exist, that it's a media creation. And yet substantial funds have been allocated to it and tens of thousands of troops are being mobilized for it. Though the theatre of war is in the jungles of central India, it will have serious consequences for us all.

If ghosts are the lingering spirits of someone or something that has ceased to exist, then perhaps the National Mineral Development Corporation's new four-lane highway crashing through the forest is the opposite of a ghost. Perhaps it is the harbinger of what is still to come.

The antagonists in the forest are disparate and unequal in almost every way. On one side is a massive paramilitary force armed with the money, the firepower, the media, and the hubris of an emerging Superpower. On the other, ordinary villagers armed with traditional weapons, backed by a superbly organized, hugely motivated Maoist guerrilla fighting force with an extraordinary and violent history of armed rebellion. The Maoists and the paramilitary are old adversaries and have fought older avatars of each other several times before: Telangana in the '50s, West Bengal, Bihar, Srikakulam in Andhra Pradesh in the late '60s and '70s, and then again in Andhra Pradesh, Bihar and Maharashtra from the

DANDAKARANYA, CENTRAL INDIA, 2010

Across the Indravati River, in the area controlled by the Maoists, is the place the police call 'Pakistan'. There the villages are empty, but the forest is full of people.

SLEEPING COMRADE

There is a spare beauty about the
place. Everything is clean
and necessary. No clutter.
A black hen parades up and
down the low mud wall.
A bamboo grid stabilizes the
rafters of the thatched roof and
doubles as a storage rack. There's
a stack of flattened, empty,
corrugated cardboard boxes.
Something catches my eye. Here's
what's printed on the cardboard:
Ideal Power 90 High Energy
Emulsion Explosive.

'80s all the way through to the present. They are familiar with each other's tactics, and have studied each other's combat manuals closely. Each time, it seemed as though the Maoists (or their previous avatars) had been not just defeated, but literally, physically exterminated. Each time, they have re-emerged, more organized, more determined and more influential than ever. Today the insurrection has spread through the mineral-rich forests of Chhattisgarh, Jharkhand, Orissa and West Bengal—homeland to millions of India's tribal people, dreamland to the corporate world.

It's easier on the liberal conscience to believe that the war in the forests is a war between the Government of India and the Maoists, who call elections a sham, Parliament a pigsty and have openly declared their intention to overthrow the Indian State. It's convenient to forget that tribal people in central India have a history of resistance that predates Mao by centuries. (That's a truism of course. If they didn't, they wouldn't exist.) The Ho, the Oraon, the Kols, the Santhals, the Mundas and the Gonds have all rebelled several times, against the British, against zamindars and moneylenders. The rebellions were cruelly crushed, many thousands killed, but the people were never conquered. Even after Independence, tribal people were at the heart of the first uprising that could be described as Maoist, in Naxalbari village in West Bengal (where the word 'Naxalite'—now used interchangeably with 'Maoist'—originates). Since then Naxalite politics has been inextricably entwined with tribal uprisings, which says as much about the tribals as it does about Naxalites.

This legacy of rebellion has left behind a furious people who have been deliberately isolated and marginalized by the Indian government. The Indian Constitution, the moral underpinning of Indian democracy, was adopted by Parliament in 1950. It was a tragic day for tribal people. The Constitution ratified colonial policy and made the state custodian of tribal homelands. Overnight, it turned the entire tribal population into squatters on their own land. It denied them their traditional rights to forest produce, it criminalized a whole way of life. In exchange for the right to vote it snatched away their right to livelihood and dignity.

Having dispossessed them and pushed them into a downward spiral of indigence, in a cruel sleight of hand, the government began to use their own penury against them. Each time it needed to displace a large population—for dams, irrigation projects, mines—it talked of 'bringing tribals into the mainstream' or of giving them 'the fruits of modern development'. Of the tens of millions of internally displaced people (more than thirty million by big dams alone), refugees of India's 'progress', the great majority are tribal people. When the government begins to talk of tribal welfare, it's time to worry.

The most recent expression of concern has come from the Home Minister P. Chidambaram, who says he doesn't want tribal people living in 'museum cultures'. The well-being of tribal people didn't seem to be such a priority during his career as a lawyer, representing the interests of several major mining companies. So it might be an idea to inquire into the basis for his new anxiety.

Over the past five years or so, the governments of Chhattisgarh, Jharkhand, Orissa and West Bengal have signed hundreds of MoUs with corporate houses, worth several billion rupees, all of them secret, for steel plants, sponge-iron factories, power plants, aluminium refineries, dams and mines. In order for the MoUs to translate into real money, tribal people must be moved.

Therefore, this war.

When a country that calls itself a democracy openly declares war within its borders, what does that war look like? Does the resistance stand a chance? Should it? Who are the Maoists? Are they just violent nihilists foisting an outdated ideology on tribal people, goading them into a hopeless insurrection? What lessons have they learned from their past experience? Is armed struggle intrinsically undemocratic? Is the Sandwich Theory—of 'ordinary' tribals being caught in the crossfire between the State and the Maoists—an accurate one? Are 'Maoists' and 'tribals' two entirely discrete categories as is being made out?

Do their interests converge? Have they learned anything from each other? Have they changed each other?

~

The day before I left, my mother called sounding sleepy. 'I've been thinking,' she said, with a mother's weird instinct, 'what this country needs is revolution.'

An article on the Internet says that Israel's Mossad is training thirty high-ranking Indian police officers in the techniques of targeted assassinations, to render the Maoist organization 'headless'.[1] There's talk in the press about the new hardware that has been bought from Israel: laser range finders, thermal imaging equipment and unmanned drones so popular with the US army. Perfect weapons to use against the poor.

~

The drive from Raipur to Dantewada takes about ten hours through areas known to be 'Maoist-infested'. These are not careless words. 'Infest/infestation' implies disease/pests. Diseases must be cured. Pests must be exterminated. Maoists must be wiped out. In these creeping, innocuous ways the language of genocide has entered our vocabulary.

To protect the highway, security forces have 'secured' a narrow bandwidth of forest on either side.

HUT IN A 'BORDER' VILLAGE

The writing on the wall. It's mandatory for Below Poverty Line (BPL) households. It says: I am poor/ I eat ₹2 per kg rice. And then the name of the family.

VILLAGE MILITIA

War doesn't seem to be uppermost on their minds. They have just finished a day's work, helping to build fencing around some village houses to keep the goats out of the fields. Their job is to patrol and protect a group of four or five villages and to help in the fields, clean wells or repair houses—doing whatever's needed.

Further in, it's the raj of the 'Dada log'. The Brothers. The Comrades.

On the outskirts of Raipur, a massive billboard advertises Vedanta (the company our home minister once worked with) Cancer Hospital. In Orissa, where it is mining bauxite, Vedanta is financing a university. In these creeping, innocuous ways mining corporations enter our imaginations: the Gentle Giants Who Really Care. It's called CSR, corporate social responsibility. It allows mining companies to be like the legendary actor and former chief minister NTR, who liked to play all the parts in Telugu mythologicals—the good guys and the bad guys, all at once, in the same movie. This CSR masks the outrageous economics that underpins the mining sector in India. For example, according to the recent Lokayukta Report for Karnataka, for every tonne of iron ore mined by a private company the government gets a royalty of ₹27 and the mining company makes ₹5000.[2] In the bauxite and aluminium sector the figures are even worse. We're talking about daylight robbery to the tune of billions of rupees. Enough to buy elections, governments, judges, newspapers, TV channels, NGOs and aid agencies. What's the occasional cancer hospital here or there?

I don't remember seeing Vedanta's name on the long list of MoUs signed by the Chhattisgarh government.

But I'm twisted enough to suspect that if there's a cancer hospital, there must be a flat-topped bauxite mountain somewhere.

We pass Kanker, famous for its Counter-Terrorism and Jungle Warfare College run by Brigadier B.K. Ponwar, Rumpelstiltskin of this war, charged with the task of turning corrupt, sloppy policemen (straw) into jungle commandos (gold). 'Fight a guerrilla like a guerrilla', the motto of the warfare training school, is painted on the rocks. The men are taught to run, slither, jump on and off airborne helicopters, ride horses (for some reason), eat snakes and live off the jungle.[3] The brigadier takes great pride in training street dogs to fight 'terrorists'. Eight hundred policemen graduate from the warfare college every six weeks. Twenty similar schools are being planned all over India. The police force is gradually being turned into an army. (In Kashmir it's the other way around. The army is being turned into a corrupt, administrative police force.) Upside down. Inside out. Either way, the Enemy is the People.

It's late. Jagdalpur is asleep, except for the many hoardings of Rahul Gandhi asking people to join the Youth Congress. He's been to Bastar twice in recent months but hasn't said anything much about the war. It's probably too messy for the People's Prince to meddle in at this point. His media managers must have put their

49

foot down. The fact that the Salwa Judum (Purification Hunt)—the dreaded government-sponsored vigilante group responsible for rapes, killings, burning down villages and driving hundreds of thousands of people from their homes—is led by Mahendra Karma, a Congress MLA, doesn't get much play in the carefully orchestrated publicity around Rahul Gandhi.

I arrived at the Ma Danteshwari mandir well in time for my appointment (first day, first show). I had my camera, my small coconut and a powdery red tika on my forehead. I wondered if someone was watching me and having a laugh. Within minutes a young boy approached me. He had a cap and a backpack schoolbag. Chipped red nail polish on his fingernails. No Hindi *Outlook*, no bananas. 'Are you the one who's going in?' he asked me. No 'Namashkar Guruji'. I didn't know what to say. He took out a soggy note from his pocket and handed it to me. It said, 'Outlook *nahi mila*' (Couldn't find *Outlook*).

'And the bananas?'

'I ate them,' he said. 'I got hungry.'

He really was a security threat.

His backpack said *Charlie Brown—Not your ordinary blockhead*. He said his name was Mangtu. I soon learned that Dandakaranya, the forest I was about to enter, was full of people who had many names and fluid identities. It was like balm to me, that idea. How lovely not to be stuck with yourself, to become someone else for a while.

We walked to the bus stand, only a few minutes away from the temple. It was already crowded. Things happened quickly. There were two men on motorbikes. There was no conversation—just a glance of acknowledgement, a shifting of body weight, the revving of engines. I had no idea where we were going. We passed the house of the superintendent of police (SP), which I recognized from my last visit. He was a candid man, the SP: 'See, ma'am, frankly speaking this problem can't be solved by us police or military. The problem with these tribals is they don't understand greed. Unless they become greedy there's no hope for us. I have told my boss, remove the force and instead put a TV in every home. Everything will be automatically sorted out.'

In no time at all we were riding out of town. No tail. It was a long ride, three hours by my watch. It ended abruptly in the middle of nowhere, on an empty road with forest on either side. Mangtu got off. I did too. The bikes left, and I picked up my backpack and followed the small internal security challenge into the forest. It was a beautiful day. The forest floor was a carpet of gold.

In a while we emerged on the white, sandy banks of a broad, flat river. It was obviously monsoon-fed, so now it was more or less a sand flat, at the centre a stream, ankle-deep, easy to wade across. Across was 'Pakistan'.

'Out there, ma'am,' the candid SP had said to me, 'my boys shoot to kill.' I remembered that as we began to cross. I saw us in a policeman's rifle-sights—tiny figures in a landscape, easy to pick off. But Mangtu seemed quite unconcerned, and I took my cue from him.

Waiting for us on the other bank, in a lime-green shirt that said *Horlicks!*, was Chandu. A slightly older security threat. Maybe twenty. He had a ready smile, a cycle, a jerry can with boiled water and many packets of glucose biscuits for me, from the Party. We caught our breath and began to walk again. The cycle, it turned out, was a red herring. The route was almost entirely non-cycle-able. We climbed steep hills and clambered down rocky paths along some pretty precarious ledges. When he couldn't wheel it, Chandu lifted the cycle and carried it over his head as though it weighed nothing. I began to wonder about his bemused village-boy air. I discovered (much later) that he could handle every kind of weapon, 'except for an LMG', he informed me cheerfully.

Three beautiful, sozzled men with flowers in their turbans walked with us for about half an hour, before our paths diverged. At sunset, their shoulder bags began to crow. They had roosters in them, which they had taken to market but hadn't managed to sell.

Chandu seems to be able to see in the dark. I have to use my torch. The crickets start up and soon there's an orchestra, a dome of sound over us. I long to look up at the night sky, but I dare not. I have to keep my eyes on the ground. One step at a time. Concentrate.

I hear dogs. But I can't tell how far away they are. The terrain flattens out. I steal a look at the sky. It makes me ecstatic. I hope we're going to stop soon. 'Soon,' Chandu says. It turns out to be more than an hour. I see silhouettes of enormous trees. We arrive.

The village seems spacious, the houses far away from each other. The house we enter is beautiful. There's a fire, some people sitting around. More people outside, in the dark. I can't tell how many. I can just about make them out. A murmur goes around. *Lal Salaam Kaamraid* (Red Salute, Comrade). 'Lal Salaam,' I say. I'm beyond tired. The lady of the house calls me inside and gives me chicken curry cooked in green beans and some red rice. Her baby is asleep next to me; her silver anklets gleam in the firelight.

After dinner I unzip my sleeping bag. It's a strange intrusive sound, the big zip. Someone puts on the radio. BBC Hindi service. The Church of England has withdrawn its funds from Vedanta's Niyamgiri project, citing environmental degradation and rights violations of the Dongria Kondh tribe. I can hear cowbells, snuffling, shuffling, cattle-farting. All's well with the world. My eyes close.

We're up at five. On the move by six. In another couple of hours, we cross another river. Every village we walk through has a family of tamarind trees watching over it, like a clutch of huge, benevolent gods. Sweet Bastar tamarind. By eleven the sun is high, and walking is less fun. We stop at a village for lunch. Chandu seems to know the people in the house. A lovely young girl flirts with him. He looks a little shy, maybe because I'm around. Lunch is raw papaya with masoor dal, and red rice. And red chilli powder. We're going to wait for the sun to lose some of its vehemence before we start walking again. We take a nap in the gazebo. There is a spare beauty about the place. Everything is clean and necessary. No clutter. A black hen parades up and down the low mud wall. A bamboo grid stabilizes the rafters of the thatched roof and doubles as a storage rack. There's a grass broom, two drums, a woven reed basket, a broken umbrella and a whole stack of flattened, empty, corrugated cardboard boxes. Something catches my eye. I need my spectacles. Here's what's printed on the cardboard: Ideal Power 90 High Energy Emulsion Explosive (Class-2) SD CAT ZZ.

We start walking again at about two. In the village we are going to we will meet a Didi (Sister, Comrade) who knows what the next step of the journey will be. Chandu doesn't. There is an economy of information too.

Nobody is supposed to know everything. But when we reach the village, Didi isn't there. There's no news of her. For the first time I see a little cloud of worry settling over Chandu. A big one settles over me. I don't know what the systems of communication are, but what if they've gone wrong?

We're parked outside a deserted school building, a little way out of the village. Why are all the government village schools built like concrete bastions, with steel shutters for windows and sliding folding steel doors? Why not like the village houses, with mud and thatch? Because they double up as barracks and bunkers. 'In the villages in Abujhmad,' Chandu says, 'schools are like this ...' He scratches a building plan with a twig in the earth. Three octagons attached to each other like a honeycomb. 'So they can fire in all directions.' He draws arrows to illustrate his point, like a cricket graphic— a batsman's wagon wheel. There are no teachers in any of the schools, Chandu says. They've all run away. Or have you

Against the greatest odds it has forged a blueprint for its own survival. It needs help and imagination. It does not need war.

chased them away? No, we only chase police. But why should teachers come here, to the jungle, when they get their salaries sitting at home? Good point.

He informs me that this is a 'new area'. The Party has entered only recently.

About twenty young people arrive, girls and boys. In their teens and early twenties. Chandu explains that this is the village-level militia, the lowest rung of the Maoists' military hierarchy. I have never seen anyone like them before. They are dressed in saris and lungis, some in frayed olive-green fatigues. The boys wear jewellery, headgear. Every one of them has a muzzle-loading rifle, what's called a *bharmaar*. Some also have knives, axes, a bow and arrow. One boy carries a crude mortar fashioned out of a heavy three-foot galvanized iron pipe. It's filled with gunpowder and shrapnel and ready to be fired. It makes a big noise, but can only be used once. Still, it scares the police, they say, and giggle. War doesn't seem to be uppermost on their minds. Perhaps because their area is outside the home range of the Salwa Judum. They have just finished a day's work, helping to build fencing around some village houses to keep the goats out of the fields. They're full of fun and curiosity. The girls are confident and easy with the boys. I have a sensor for this sort of thing, and I am impressed. Their job, Chandu says, is to patrol and protect a group of four or five villages and to help in the fields, clean wells or repair houses—doing whatever's needed.

Still no Didi. What to do? Nothing. Wait. Help out with some chopping and peeling.

After dinner, without much talk, everybody falls in line. Clearly we're moving. Everything moves with us, the rice, vegetables, pots and pans. We leave the school compound and walk single file into the forest. In less than half an hour we arrive in a glade where we are going to sleep. There's absolutely no noise. Within minutes everyone has spread their blue plastic sheets, the ubiquitous *jhilli* (without which there will be no Revolution). Chandu and Mangtu share one and spread one out for me. They find me the best place, by the best grey rock. Chandu says he has sent a message to Didi. If she gets it she will be here first thing in the morning. *If* she gets it.

It's the most beautiful room I have slept in in a long time. My private suite in a thousand-star hotel. I'm surrounded by these strange, beautiful children with their curious arsenal. They're all Maoists for sure. Are they all going to die? Is the Jungle Warfare College for them? And the helicopter gunships, the thermal imaging and the laser range finders?

Why must they die? What for? To turn all of this into a mine? I remember my visit to the opencast iron-

MAOIST BANNER IN THE FOREST
'Stop India from becoming the grazing ground of Imperialism. The Central Government has no right to ask for our votes. Do not vote for those millionaires who are getting rich by selling off our wealth. Fight for self-reliant, revolutionary development. Boycott the Lok Sabha elections.'

THE LONG MARCH

We're moving in single file now. Myself, and one hundred 'senselessly violent', bloodthirsty insurgents.

ore mines in Keonjhar, Orissa. There was forest there once. And children like these. Now the land is like a raw, red wound. Red dust fills your nostrils and lungs. The water is red, the air is red, the people are red, their lungs and hair are red. All day and all night trucks rumble through their villages, bumper to bumper, thousands and thousands of trucks, taking ore to Paradip port from where it will go to China. There it will turn into cars and smoke and sudden cities that spring up overnight. Into a 'growth rate' that leaves economists breathless. Into weapons to make war.

Everyone's asleep except for the sentries who take one-and-a-half-hour shifts. Finally I can look at the stars. When I was a child growing up on the banks of the Meenachal River, I used to think the sound of crickets— which always started up at twilight—was the sound of stars revving up, getting ready to shine. I'm surprised at how much I love being here. There is nowhere else in the world that I would rather be. Who should I be tonight? Kaamraid Rahel, under the stars? Maybe Didi will come tomorrow.

They arrive in the early afternoon. I can see them from a distance. About fifteen of them, all in olive-green uniforms, running towards us. Even from a distance, from the *way* they run, I can tell they are the heavy hitters. The People's Liberation Guerrilla Army (PLGA).

For whom the thermal imaging and laser guided rifles. For whom the Jungle Warfare College.

They carry serious rifles, INSAS, SLR; two have AK-47s. The leader of the squad is Comrade Madhav who has been with the Party since he was nine. He's from Warangal, Andhra Pradesh. He's upset and extremely apologetic. There was a major miscommunication, he says again and again, which usually *never* happens. I was supposed to have arrived at the main camp on the very first night. Someone dropped the baton in the jungle-relay. The motorcycle drop was to have been at an entirely different place. 'We made you wait, we made you walk so much. We ran all the way when the message came that you were here.' I said it was OK, that I had come prepared, to wait and walk and listen. He wants to leave immediately, because people in the camp were waiting, and worried.

It's a few hours' walk to the camp. It's getting dark when we arrive. There are several layers of sentries and concentric circles of patrolling. There must be a hundred comrades lined up in two rows. Everyone has a weapon. And a smile. They begin to sing: *Lal lal salaam, lal lal salaam, aane vaaley saathiyon ko lal lal salaam.* (Red salute to the comrades who have arrived.) It was sung sweetly, as though it was a folk song about a river, or a forest blossom. With the song, the greeting, the handshake and the clenched fist. Everyone greets everyone, murmuring *Lalslaam, mlalslaa mlalslaam* …

Other than a large blue jhilli spread out on the floor, about fifteen feet square, there are no signs of a 'camp'. This one has a jhilli roof as well. It's my room for the night. I was either being rewarded for my days of walking, or being pampered in advance for what lay ahead. Or both. Either way it was the last time in the entire trip that I was going to have a roof over my head. Over dinner I meet Comrade Narmada, in charge of the Krantikari Adivasi Mahila Sangathan (KAMS), who has a price on her head; Comrade Saroja of the PLGA, who is only as tall as her SLR; Comrade Maase (which means Black Girl in Gondi), who has a price on her head too; Comrade Roopi, the tech wizard; Comrade Raju, who's in charge of the division I'd been walking through; and Comrade Venu (or Murali or Sonu or Sushil, whatever you would like to call him), clearly the seniormost of them all. Maybe Central Committee, maybe even Politburo. I'm not told, I don't ask. Between us we speak Gondi, Halbi, Telugu, Punjabi and Malayalam. Only Maase speaks English. (So we all communicate in Hindi!) Comrade Maase is tall and quiet and seems to have to swim through a layer of pain to enter the conversation. But from the way she hugs me I can tell she's a reader. And that she misses having books in the jungle. She will tell me her story only later. When she trusts me with her grief.

Bad news arrives, as it does in this jungle. A runner, with 'biscuits'. Handwritten notes on sheets of paper, folded and stapled into little squares. There's a bag full of them. Like chips. News from everywhere. The police have killed five people in Ongnaar village, four from the militia and one ordinary villager: Santhu Pottai (25), Phoolo Vadde (22), Kande Pottai (22), Ramoli Vadde (20), Dalsai Koram (22). They could have been the children in my star-spangled dormitory of last night.

Then good news arrives. A small contingent of people with a plump young man. He's in fatigues too, but they look brand new. Everybody admires them and comments on the fit. He looks shy and pleased. He's a doctor who has come to live and work with the comrades in the forest. The last time a doctor visited Dandakaranya was many years ago.

On the radio there's news about the home minister's meeting with chief ministers of states affected by 'left-wing extremism'. The chief ministers of Jharkhand and Bihar are being demure and have not attended. Everybody sitting around the radio laughs. Around the time of elections, they say, right through the campaign, and then maybe a month or two after the government is formed, mainstream politicians all say things like 'Naxals are our children'. You can set your watch to the schedule of when they will change their minds, and grow fangs.

I am introduced to Comrade Kamla. I am told that I must on no account go even five feet away from my jhilli without waking her. Because everybody gets disoriented in the dark and could get seriously lost. (I don't wake her. I sleep like a log.) In the morning Kamla presents me with a yellow polythene packet with one corner snipped off. Once it used to contain Abis Gold Refined Soya Oil. Now it was my Loo Mug. Nothing's wasted on the Road to the Revolution.

(Even now I think of Comrade Kamla all the time, every day. She's seventeen. She wears a homemade pistol on her hip. And boy, what a smile. But if the police come across her, they will kill her. They might rape her first. No questions will be asked. Because she's an Internal Security Challenge.)

After breakfast Comrade Venu (Sushil, Sonu, Murali) is waiting for me, sitting cross-legged on the jhilli, looking for all the world like a frail village schoolteacher. I'm going to get a history lesson. Or, more accurately, a lecture on the history of the last thirty years in the Dandakaranya forest, which has culminated in the war that's swirling through it today. For sure, it's a partisan's version. But then, what history isn't? In any case, the secret history must be made public if it is to be contested, argued with, instead of merely being lied about, which is what is happening now.

Comrade Venu has a calm, reassuring manner and a gentle voice that will, in the days to come, surface in a context that will completely unnerve me. This morning he talks for several hours, almost continuously. He's like a little store manager who has a giant bunch of keys with which to open up a maze of lockers full of stories, songs and insights.

Comrade Venu was in one of the seven armed squads that crossed the Godavari from Andhra Pradesh and entered the Dandakaranya forest (DK, in Partyspeak) in June 1980, thirty years ago. He is one of the original forty-niners. They belonged to the People's War Group (PWG), a faction of the Communist Party of India (Marxist-Leninist), CPI (ML), the original Naxalites. PWG was formally announced as a separate, independent party in April that year, under Kondapalli Seetharamiah. PWG had decided to build a standing army, for which it would need a base. DK was to be that base, and those first squads were sent in to reconnoitre the area and begin the process of building guerrilla zones. The debate about whether Communist parties ought to have a standing army, and whether or not a 'people's army' is a contradiction in terms, is an old one. PWG's decision to build an army came from its experience in Andhra

65

A COMRADE FROM THE
PEOPLE'S LIBERATION
GUERRILLA ARMY (PLGA)
The PLGA was formally
constituted in December 2000.
It is an entirely voluntary army.
Nobody is paid a salary.
Women constitute 45 per cent
of its cadre.

CAMP

I looked around at the camp before we left. There are no signs that almost a hundred people had camped here, except for some ash where the fires had been. I cannot believe this army. As far as consumption goes, it's more Gandhian than any Gandhian, and has a lighter carbon footprint than any climate change evangelist.

Pradesh, where its 'Land to the Tiller' campaign led to a direct clash with the landlords, and resulted in the kind of police repression that the Party found impossible to withstand without a trained fighting force of its own.

By 2004 PWG had merged with the other CPI (ML) factions, Party Unity (PU) and the Maoist Communist Centre (MCC)—which functions for the most part out of Bihar and Jharkhand—to become what it is now, the Communist Party of India (Maoist).

~

Dandakaranya is part of what the British, in their White Man's way, called Gondwana, land of the Gonds. Today the state boundaries of Madhya Pradesh, Chhattisgarh, Orissa, Andhra Pradesh and Maharashtra slice through the forest. Breaking up a troublesome people into separate administrative units is an old trick. But these Gonds and Maoists and Maoist Gonds don't pay much attention to things like state boundaries. They have different maps in their heads and, like other creatures of the forest, they have their own paths. For them, roads are not meant for walking on. They're meant only to be crossed or, as is increasingly becoming the case, ambushed. Though the Gonds (divided between the Koya and Dorla tribes) are by far the biggest majority, there are small settlements of other tribal communities too. The non-adivasi communities, traders and settlers, live on the edges of the forest, near the roads and markets.

The PWG were not the first evangelicals to arrive in Dandakaranya. Baba Amte, the well-known Gandhian, had opened his ashram and leprosy hospital in Warora in 1975.[4] The Ramakrishna Mission and the Gayatri Samaj had begun opening village schools in the remote forests of Abujhmad. In north Bastar, Baba Bihari Das had started an aggressive drive to 'bring tribals back into the Hindu fold', which involved a campaign to denigrate tribal culture, induce self-hatred, and introduce Hinduism's great gift—caste. The first converts, the village chiefs and big landlords—people like Mahendra Karma, founder of the Salwa Judum—were conferred the status of Dwij, twice-born, Brahmins. (Of course this was a bit of a scam, because nobody can *become* a Brahmin. If they could, we'd be a nation of Brahmins by now.) But this counterfeit Hinduism is considered good enough for tribal people, just like the counterfeit brands of everything else—biscuits, soap, matches, oil— that are sold in village markets. As part of the Hindutva drive the names of villages were changed in land records, as a result of which most have two names now, people's names and government names. Innar village, for example, became Chinnari. On voters' lists tribal names were changed to Hindu names. (Massa Karma became

69

Mahendra Karma.) Those who did not come forward to join the Hindu fold were declared 'Katwas' (by which they meant Untouchables), who later became the natural constituency for the Maoists.

The PWG first began work in south Bastar and Gadchiroli. Comrade Venu describes those first months in some detail: how the villagers were suspicious of them, and wouldn't let them into their homes. No one would offer them food or water. The police spread rumours that they were thieves. The women hid their jewellery in the ashes of their wood stoves. There was an enormous amount of repression. In November 1980, in Gadchiroli the police opened fire at a village meeting and killed Peddi Shankar, a squad member. He was the Party's first 'martyr' in DK. It was a traumatic setback, and the comrades retreated across the Godavari and returned to Adilabad.

But in 1981 they returned. They began to organize tribal people to demand a rise in the price they were being paid for tendu leaves (which are used to make beedis). At the time, traders paid 3 paise for a bundle of about fifty leaves. It was a formidable job to organize people entirely unfamiliar with this kind of politics, to lead them on strike. Eventually the strike was successful and the price was doubled, to 6 paise a bundle. But the real success for the Party was to have been able to demonstrate the value of unity and a new way of conducting a political negotiation. Today, after several strikes and agitations, the price of a bundle of tendu leaves is ₹1. (It seems a little improbable at these rates, but the turnover of the tendu business runs into hundreds of millions of rupees.) Every season the government floats tenders and gives contractors permission to extract a fixed volume of tendu leaves—usually between 1500 and 5000 standard bags known as *manak boras*. Each manak bora contains about 1000 bundles. (Of course there's no way of ensuring that the contractors don't extract more than they're meant to.) By the time the tendu enters the market it is sold in kilos. The slippery arithmetic and the sly system of measurement that converts bundles into manak boras into kilos is controlled by the contractors, and leaves plenty of room for manipulation of the worst kind. The most conservative estimate puts their profit per standard bag at about ₹1100. (That's after paying the Party a 'levy' of ₹120 per bag.) Even by that gauge, a small contractor (1500 bags) makes about ₹1.6 million a season and a big one (5000 bags) up to ₹5.5 million. A more realistic estimate would be several times this amount. Meanwhile those who do the actual work make just enough to stay alive until the next season.

We're interrupted by some laughter and the sight of Nilesh, one of the young PLGA comrades, walking rapidly towards the cooking area, slapping himself. When he comes closer I see that he's carrying a leafy nest of angry red ants that have crawled all over him and are biting him on his arms and neck. Nilesh is laughing too. 'Have you ever eaten ant chutney?' Comrade Venu asks me. I know these red ants well, from my childhood in Kerala, I've been bitten by them, but I've never eaten them. (The chutney turns out to be nice. Sour. Lots of formic acid.)

Nilesh is from Bijapur, which is at the heart of Salwa Judum operations. Nilesh's younger brother joined the Judum on one of its looting and burning sprees and was made a Special Police Officer (SPO). He lives in the Basaguda camp with his mother. His father refused to go and stayed behind in the village. In effect, it's a family blood feud. Later on when I had an opportunity to talk to him I asked Nilesh why his brother had done that. 'He was very young,' Nilesh said. 'He got an opportunity to run wild and hurt people and burn houses. He went crazy, did terrible things. Now he is stuck. He can never come back to the village. He will not be forgiven. He knows that.'

~

We return to the history lesson. The Party's next big struggle, Comrade Venu says, was against the

Ballarpur Paper Mills. The government had given its owners, the Thapars, a forty-five-year contract to extract 150,000 tonnes of bamboo at a hugely subsidized rate. (Small beer compared to bauxite, but still.) The tribals were paid 10 paise for a bundle that contained twenty culms of bamboo. (I won't yield to the vulgar temptation of comparing that with the profits the Thapars were making.) A long agitation, a strike, followed by negotiations with officials of the paper mill in the presence of the people, tripled the price to 30 paise per bundle. For the tribal people these were huge achievements. Other political parties had made promises, but showed no signs of keeping them. People began to approach the PWG asking whether they could join up.

But the politics of tendu, bamboo and other forest produce was seasonal. The perennial problem, the real bane of people's lives, was the biggest landlord of all, the Forest Department. Every morning forest officials, even the most junior of them, would appear in villages like a bad dream, preventing people from ploughing their fields, grazing their cattle, collecting firewood, plucking leaves, picking fruit—from *living*. They brought elephants to overrun fields and scattered babool seeds to destroy the soil as they passed by. People would be beaten, arrested, humiliated, their crops destroyed. Of course, from the Forest Department's point of view, these were illegal people engaged in unconstitutional activity, and the department was only implementing the Rule of Law. (Their sexual exploitation of women was just an added perk in a hardship posting.)

Emboldened by the people's participation in these struggles, the Party decided to confront the Forest Department. It encouraged people to take over forest land and cultivate it. The Forest Department retaliated by burning new villages that came up in forest areas. In 1986 it announced a National Park in Bijapur, which meant the eviction of sixty villages. More than half of them had already been moved out and construction of National Park infrastructure had begun when the Party moved in. It demolished the construction and stopped the eviction of the remaining villages. It prevented the Forest Department from entering the area. On a few occasions, officials were captured, tied to trees and beaten by villagers. It was cathartic revenge for generations of exploitation. Eventually the Forest Department fled. Between 1986 and 2000, the Party redistributed 300,000 acres (1214 square kilometres) of forest land. Today, Comrade Venu says, there are no landless peasants in Dandakaranya.

For today's generation of young people, the Forest Department is a distant memory, the stuff of stories mothers tell their children, about a mythological past of bondage and humiliation. For the older generation, freedom from the Forest Department meant genuine freedom. They could touch it, taste it. It meant far more than India's Independence ever did. They began to rally to the Party that had struggled with them.

The seven-squad team had come a long way. Its influence now ranged across a 60,000-square-kilometre stretch of forest, thousands of villages and millions of people.

But the departure of the Forest Department heralded the arrival of the police. That set off a cycle of bloodshed. Fake 'encounters' by the police, ambushes by the PWG. With the redistribution of land came other responsibilities: irrigation, agricultural productivity, and the problem of an expanding population arbitrarily clearing forest land. A decision was taken to separate 'mass work' and 'military work'.

Today, Dandakaranya is administered by an elaborate structure of Janatana Sarkars (people's governments). The organizing principles came from the Chinese revolution and the national liberation struggle in Vietnam. Each Janatana Sarkar is elected by a cluster of villages whose combined population can range from 500 to 5000. It has nine departments: Krishi (agriculture), Vyapar-Udyog (trade and industry), Arthik

JANATANA SARKAR FLAG

Today Dandakaranya is administered by an elaborate system of Janatana Sarkars (people's governments). Each Janatana Sarkar is elected by a cluster of villages. It has nine departments, 'We have a Save the Jungle department now,' Comrade Venu says.

COMRADE KAMLA
SHOWS OFF JANATANA
SARKAR FIELDS

It's not an Alternative yet, this idea of Gram Swaraj with a Gun. There is too much hunger, too much sickness here. But it has certainly created the possibilities for an alternative. Not for the whole world, not for Alaska, or New Delhi, nor even perhaps for the whole of Chhattisgarh, but for itself. For Dandakaranya.

(economic), Nyay (justice), Raksha (defence), Hospital (health), Jan Sampark (public relations), School–Riti Rivaj (education and culture) and Jungle. A group of Janatana Sarkars come under an Area Committee. Three Area Committees make up a Division. There are ten Divisions in Dandakaranya.

'We have a Save the Jungle department now,' Comrade Venu says. 'You must have read the government report that says forest has increased in Naxal areas?'

Ironically, Comrade Venu says, the first people to benefit from the Party's campaign against the Forest Department were the Mukhiyas (village chiefs)—the Dwij brigade. They used their manpower and their resources to grab as much land as they could, while the going was good. But then people began to approach the Party with their 'internal contradictions', as Comrade Venu puts it quaintly. The Party began to turn its attention to issues of equity, class and injustice *within* tribal society. The big landlords sensed trouble on the horizon. As the Party's influence expanded, theirs had begun to wane. Increasingly people were taking their problems to the Party instead of to the Mukhiyas. Old forms of exploitation began to be challenged. On the day of the first rain, people were traditionally supposed to till the Mukhiyas' land instead of their own. That stopped. They no longer offered them the first day's picking of mahua or other forest produce.

Obviously, something needed to be done.

Enter Mahendra Karma, one of the biggest landlords in the region and at the time a member of the Communist Party of India (CPI). In 1990 he rallied a group of Mukhiyas and landlords and started a campaign called the Jan Jagran Abhiyan (Public Awakening Campaign). Their way of 'awakening' the 'public' was to form a hunting party of about 300 men to comb the forest, killing people, burning houses and molesting women. The then Madhya Pradesh government—Chhattisgarh had not yet been created—provided police backup. In Maharashtra, something similar, called 'Democratic Front', began its assault. People's War responded to all of this in true People's War style, by killing a few of the most notorious landlords. In a few months the Jan Jagran Abhiyan, the 'white terror'—Comrade Venu's term for it—faded. In 1998 Mahendra Karma, who had by now joined the Congress party, tried to revive the Jan Jagran Abhiyan. This time it fizzled out even faster than before.

Then, in the summer of 2005, fortune favoured him. In April the Bharatiya Janata Party (BJP) government in Chhattisgarh signed two MoUs to set up integrated steel plants (the terms of which are secret). One for ₹70 billion with Essar Steel in Bailadila, and the other for ₹100 billion with Tata Steel in Lohandiguda. It was around then that Prime Minister Manmohan Singh was making his now famous statement about the Maoists being the 'biggest internal security challenge' to India.[5] (It was an odd thing to say at the time, because actually the opposite was true. The Congress government in Andhra Pradesh had just outmanoeuvred the Maoists, decimated them. They had lost about 1600 of their cadre and were in complete disarray.) The PM's statement sent the share-value of mining companies soaring. It also sent a signal to the media that the Maoists were fair game for anyone who chose to go after them. In June 2005, Mahendra Karma called a secret meeting of Mukhiyas in Kutroo village and announced the Salwa Judum (Purification Hunt). A lovely mélange of tribal earthiness and Dwij/Nazi sentiment.

Unlike the Jan Jagran Abhiyan, the Salwa Judum was a ground-clearing operation, meant to move people out of their villages into roadside camps, where they could be policed and controlled. In military terms, it's called Strategic Hamleting. It was devised by General Sir Harold Briggs in 1950 when the British were at war against the Communists in Malaya. The Briggs Plan became very popular with the Indian Army, which has used it in Nagaland, Mizoram and in Telangana. The BJP chief minister of Chhattisgarh, Raman Singh, announced that as far as his government was concerned, villagers who did not move into camps would be considered

Maoists. So in Bastar, for an ordinary villager, just staying at home, living an ordinary life, became the equivalent of indulging in dangerous terrorist activity.

Along with a steel mug of black tea, as a special treat, someone hands me a pair of earphones and switches on a little MP3 player. It's a scratchy recording of the then SP Bijapur, D.S. Manhar, briefing a junior officer over the wireless about the rewards and incentives the state and central governments are offering to 'jagrit' (awakened) villages, and to people who agree to move into camps. He then gives clear instructions that villages that refuse to 'surrender' should be burnt and journalists who want to cover Naxalites should be shot on sight. (I'd read about this in the papers long ago. When the story broke, rumour has it that as punishment—it's not clear to whom—the SP was transferred to the State Human Rights Commission.)

The Salwa Judum was announced at a meeting of village Mukhiyas in a village called Ambeli in June 2005. Between June and December 2005, it burned, killed, raped and looted its way through hundreds of villages of south Dantewada. The centre of its operations were the Bijapur and Bhairamgarh blocks near Bailadila, where Essar Steel's new plant was proposed. Not coincidentally, these were also Maoist strongholds, where the Janatana Sarkars had done a great deal of work, especially in building water-harvesting structures. The Janatana Sarkars became the special target of the Salwa Judum's attacks. Hundreds of people were killed in the most brutal ways. About 60,000 people moved into the camps, some voluntarily, others out of terror. Of these, about 3000 were appointed Special Police Officers on a salary of ₹1500.

For these paltry crumbs, young people, like Nilesh's brother, have sentenced themselves to life in a barbed-wire enclosure. Cruel as they have been, they could end up being the worst victims of this horrible war. No Supreme Court judgement ordering the Salwa Judum to be dismantled can change their fate.

The remaining hundreds of thousands of people went off the government radar. (But the development funds for these 644 villages did not. What happens to that little gold mine?) Many of them made their way to Andhra Pradesh and Orissa where they usually migrated to work as contract labour during the chilli-picking season. But tens of thousands fled into the forest, where they still remain, living without shelter, coming back to their fields and homes only in the daytime.

In the slipstream of the Salwa Judum, a swarm of police stations and camps appeared. The idea was to provide carpet security for a 'creeping reoccupation' of Maoist-controlled territory. The assumption was that the

Maoists would not dare to attack such a large concentration of security forces. The Maoists, for their part, realized that if they did not break that carpet security it would amount to abandoning people whose trust they had earned, and with whom they had lived and worked for twenty-five years. They struck back in a series of attacks on the heart of the security grid.

On 26 January 2006 the PLGA attacked the Gangalaur police camp and killed seven people. On 17 July 2006 the Salwa Judum camp at Erabor was attacked, twenty people were killed and 150 injured. (You might have read about it—something like 'Maoists attacked the relief camp set up by the state government to provide shelter to the villagers who had fled from their villages because of terror unleashed by the Naxalites.') On 13 December 2006 they attacked the Basaguda 'relief' camp and killed three SPOs and a constable. On 15 March 2007 came the most audacious of them all. One hundred and twenty PLGA guerrillas attacked the Rani Bodili Kanya Ashram,

Salwa Judum leader.
Dornapal Camp, 2009

a girls' hostel that had been converted into a barrack for eighty Chhattisgarh police (and SPOs) while the girls still lived in it as human shields. The PLGA entered the compound, cordoned off the annexe in which the girls lived, and attacked the barracks. Fifty-five policemen and SPOs were killed. None of the girls was hurt. (The candid SP of Dantewada had shown me his PowerPoint presentation with horrifying photographs of the burned, disembowelled bodies of the policemen amidst the ruins of the blown-up school building. They were so macabre, it was impossible not to look away. He looked pleased at my reaction.)

The attack on Rani Bodili caused an uproar in the country. Human rights organizations condemned the Maoists not just for their violence, but also for being anti-education and attacking schools. But in Dandakaranya the Rani Bodili attack became a legend: songs and poems and plays were written about it.

The Maoist counteroffensive did break the carpet security and gave people breathing space. The police and the Salwa Judum retreated into their camps, from which they now emerge—usually in the dead of night—only in packs of 300 or 1000 to carry out Cordon and Search operations in villages. Gradually, except for the SPOs and their families, the rest of the people in the Salwa Judum camps began to return to their villages. The Maoists welcomed them back and announced that even SPOs could return if they genuinely, and publicly, regretted their actions. Young people began to flock to the PLGA. (The PLGA had been formally constituted in December 2000. Over the last thirty years, its armed squads had very gradually expanded into sections, sections had grown into platoons, and platoons into companies. But after the Salwa Judum's depredations, the PLGA was rapidly able to declare battalion strength. It is an entirely voluntary army. Nobody is paid a salary.)

The Salwa Judum had not just failed, it had backfired badly.

As we now know, it was not just a local operation by a small-time hood. Regardless of the doublespeak in the press, the Salwa Judum was a joint operation by the state government of Chhattisgarh and the Congress party, which was in power at the centre. It could not be allowed to fail. Not when all those MoUs were still waiting, like wilting hopefuls on the marriage market. The government was under tremendous pressure to come up with a new plan. They came up with Operation Green Hunt. The Salwa Judum SPOs are called Koya Commandos now. It has deployed the Chhattisgarh Armed Force (CAF), the Central Reserve Police Force (CRPF), the Border Security Force (BSF), the Indo-Tibetan Border Police (ITBP), the Central Industrial

Security Force (CISF), Greyhounds, Scorpions, Cobras. And a policy that's affectionately called WHAM— Winning Hearts and Minds.

Significant wars are often fought in unlikely places. Free Market Capitalism defeated Soviet Communism in the bleak mountains of Afghanistan. Here in the forests of Dantewada a battle rages for the soul of India. Plenty has been said about the deepening crisis in Indian democracy and the collusion between big corporations, the media, major political parties and the security establishment. If anybody wants to do a quick spot check, Dantewada is the place to go.

A draft report on State Agrarian Relations and the Unfinished Task of Land Reform (Volume 1) said that Tata Steel and Essar Steel were the first financiers of the Salwa Judum. Because it was a government report, it created a flurry when it was reported in the press. (That fact has subsequently been dropped from the final report. Was it a genuine error, or did someone receive a gentle, integrated steel tap on the shoulder?)[6]

On 12 October 2009 the mandatory public hearing for Tata's steel plant, meant to be held in Lohandiguda where local people could come, actually took place in a small hall inside the Collectorate in Jagdalpur, many miles away, cordoned off with massive security. A hired audience of fifty tribals was brought in a guarded convoy of government jeeps. After the meeting the District Collector congratulated 'the people of Lohandiguda' for their cooperation. The local newspapers reported the lie, even though they knew better. (The advertisements rolled in.) Despite villagers' objections, land acquisition for the project has begun.

The Maoists are not the only ones who seek to depose the Indian State. It's already been deposed, several times, by Hindu fundamentalism and economic totalitarianism.

Lohandiguda, a five-hour drive from Dantewada, never used to be a Naxalite area. But it is now. Comrade Joori, who sat next to me while I ate the ant chutney, works in the area. She said they decided to move in after graffiti had begun to appear on the walls of village houses, saying *Naxali Ao, Hamein Bachao!* (Naxals come and save us!) A few months ago Vimal Meshram, vice-president of the janpad panchayat, was shot dead in the market. 'He was Tata's Man,' Joori says. 'He was forcing people to give up their land and accept compensation. It's good that he's been finished. D'you want more *chapoli*?' She's crunching red ants. 'We won't let the Tata come there. People don't want them.' Joori is not PLGA. She's in the Chetna Natya Manch (CNM), the cultural wing of the Party. She sings. She writes songs. She's from Abujhmad. (She's married to Comrade Madhav. She fell in love with his singing when he visited her village with a CNM troupe.)

I feel I ought to say something at this point. About the futility of violence, about the unacceptability of summary executions. But what should I suggest they do? Go to court? Do a dharna in Jantar Mantar, New Delhi? A rally? A relay hunger strike? It sounds ridiculous. The promoters of the New Economic Policy—who find it so easy to say 'There Is No Alternative'—should be asked to suggest an alternative Resistance Policy. A specific one, to these specific people, in this specific forest. Here. Now. Which party should they vote for? Which democratic institution in this country should they approach? Which door did the Narmada Bachao Andolan *not* knock on during the years and years it fought against Big Dams on the Narmada?

~

It's dark. There's a lot of activity in the camp, but I can't see anything. Just points of light moving around. It's hard to tell whether they are stars or fireflies or Maoists on the move. Little Mangtu appears from nowhere. I found out that he's one of a group of ten kids who are part of the first batch of the Young Communists Mobile School, who are being taught to read and write, and tutored in basic communist principles. ('Indoctrination of young minds!' our corporate media howls. The TV advertisements that brainwash children before they can even think are not seen as a form of indoctrination.) The young communists are not allowed to carry guns or wear uniforms. But they trail the PLGA squads, with stars in their eyes, like groupies of a rock band.

Mangtu has adopted me with a gently proprietorial air. He has filled my water bottle and says I should pack my bag. A whistle blows. The blue jhilli tent is dismantled and folded up in five minutes flat. Another whistle and all hundred comrades fall in line. Five rows. Comrade Raju is the Director of Ops. There's a roll call. I'm in the line too, shouting out my number when Comrade Kamla, who is in front of me, prompts me. (We count to twenty and then start from one, because that's as far as most adivasis count. Twenty is enough for them. Maybe it should be enough for us too.) Chandu is in fatigues now, and carries a Sten gun. In a low voice Comrade Raju is briefing the group. It's all in Gondi, I don't understand a thing, but I keep hearing the word RV. Later Raju tells me it stands for rendezvous! It's a Gondi word now. 'We make RV points so that in case we come under fire and people have to scatter, they know where to regroup.' He cannot possibly know the kind of panic this induces in me. Not because I'm scared of being fired on, but because I'm scared of being lost. I'm a directional dyslexic, capable of getting lost between my bedroom and my bathroom. What will I do in 60,000 square kilometres of forest? Come hell or high water, I'm

REST

Dandakaranya was full of people who had many names and fluid identities. It was like balm to me, that idea. How lovely not to be stuck with yourself, to become someone else for a while.

STORYTELLING

I feel I ought to say something at this point. About the futility of violence, about the unacceptability of summary executions. But what should I suggest they do? Go to court? Do a dharna in Jantar Mantar, New Delhi? Which party should they vote for? Which democratic institution in this country should they approach?

going to be holding on to Comrade Raju's pallu.

Before we start walking, Comrade Venu comes up to me. 'OK then Comrade. I'll take your leave.' I'm taken aback. He looks like a little mosquito in a woollen cap and chappals, surrounded by his guards, three women, three men. Heavily armed. 'We are very grateful to you Comrade, for coming all the way here,' he says. Once again the handshake, the clenched fist. 'Lal Salaam, Comrade.' He disappears into the forest, the Keeper of the Keys. And in a moment, it's as though he was never here. I'm a little bereft. But I have hours of recordings to listen to. And as the days turn into weeks, I will meet many people who paint colour and detail into the grid he drew for me. We begin to walk in the opposite direction. Comrade Raju, smelling of Iodex from a mile off, says with a happy smile, 'My knees are gone. I can only walk if I have had a fistful of painkillers.'

Comrade Raju speaks perfect Hindi and has a deadpan way of telling the funniest stories. He worked as an advocate in Raipur for eighteen years. Both he and his wife, Malti, were Party members and part of its city network. At the end of 2007 one of the key people in the Raipur network was arrested, tortured and eventually turned informer. He was driven around Raipur in a closed police vehicle and made to point out his former colleagues. Comrade Malti was one of them. On 22 January 2008 she was arrested along with several others. One of the charges against her is that she mailed CDs containing video evidence of Salwa Judum atrocities to several Members of Parliament. Her case rarely comes up for hearing because the police know their case is flimsy. But the new Chhattisgarh Special Public Security Act (CSPSA) allows the police to hold her without bail for several years. 'Now the government has deployed several battalions of Chhattisgarh police to protect the poor Members of Parliament from their own mail,' Comrade Raju says. He didn't get caught because he was in Dandakaranya at the time, attending a meeting. He's been here ever since. His two school-going children, who were left alone at home, were interrogated extensively by the police. Finally their home was packed up and they went to live with an uncle. Comrade Raju received news of them for the first time only a few weeks ago. What gives him this strength, this ability to hold on to his acid humour? What keeps them all going, despite all they have endured? Their faith and hope—and love—for the Party. I encounter it again and again, in the deepest, most personal ways.

~

We're moving in single file now. Myself, and one hundred 'senselessly violent', bloodthirsty insurgents. I looked around at the camp before we left. There are no signs that almost a hundred people had camped here, except for some ash where the fires had been. I cannot believe this army. As far as consumption goes, it's more Gandhian than any Gandhian, and has a lighter carbon footprint than any climate change evangelist. But for now, it even has a Gandhian approach to sabotage; before a police vehicle is burnt for example, it is stripped down and every part is cannibalized. The steering wheel is straightened out and made into a bharmaar barrel, the rexine upholstery stripped and used for ammunition pouches, the battery for solar charging. (The new instructions from the high command are that captured vehicles should be buried and not cremated. So they can be resurrected when needed.) Should I write a play I wonder—*Gandhi Get Your Gun*. Or will I be lynched?

We're walking in pitch darkness and dead silence. I'm the only one using a torch, pointed down so that all I can see in its circle of light are Comrade Kamla's bare heels in her scuffed, black chappals, showing me exactly where to put my feet. She is carrying ten times more weight than I am. Her backpack, a rifle, a huge bag of provisions on her head, one of the large cooking pots and two shoulder bags full of vegetables. The bag on her head is perfectly balanced, and she can scramble down slopes and slippery rock pathways without so much as touching it. She is a miracle. It turns out to be a long walk. I'm grateful to the history lesson because apart from everything else it gave my feet a rest for a whole day.

It's the most wonderful thing, walking in the forest at night. And I'll be doing it night after night.

~

We're going to a centenary celebration of the 1910 Bhumkal rebellion in which the Koyas rose up against the British. *Bhumkal*, Comrade Raju says, means earthquake. He says people will walk for days together to come for the celebration. The forest must be full of people on the move. There are celebrations in all the DK divisions. We are privileged because Comrade Leng, the master of ceremonies, is walking with us. In Gondi *leng* means 'the voice'. Comrade Leng is a tall, middle-aged man from Andhra Pradesh, a colleague of the legendary and beloved singer-poet Gadar, who founded the radical cultural organization Jan Natya Manch (JNM) in 1972. Eventually JNM became a formal part of the PWG and could draw audiences numbering in the tens of thousands in Andhra Pradesh. Comrade Leng joined in 1977 and became a famous singer in his own right. He lived in Andhra through the worst repression, the era of 'encounter' killings in which friends died almost every day. He himself was picked up one night from his hospital bed, by a woman superintendent of police, masquerading as a doctor. He was taken to the forest outside Warangal to be 'encountered'. But luckily for him, Comrade Leng says, Gadar got the news and managed to raise an alarm. When the PWG decided to start a cultural organization in DK in 1998, Comrade

Leng was sent to head the Chetna Natya Manch. And here he is now, walking with me, wearing an olive-green shirt and, for some reason, purple pyjamas with pink bunnies on them. 'There are 10,000 members in CNM now,' he told me. 'We have 500 songs, in Hindi, Gondi, Chhattisgarhi and Halbi. We have printed a book with 140 of our songs. Everybody writes songs.' The first time I spoke to him, he sounded very grave, very single-minded. But days later, sitting around a fire, still in those pyjamas, he tells us about a very successful, mainstream Telugu film director (a friend of his), who always plays a

Naxalite in his own films. 'I asked him,' Comrade Leng said in his lovely Telugu-accented Hindi, 'why do you think Naxalites are always like this?'—and he did a deft caricature of a crouched, high-stepping, hunted-looking man emerging from the forest with an AK-47, and left us screaming with laughter.

I'm not sure whether I'm looking forward to the Bhumkal celebrations. I fear I'll see traditional tribal dances stiffened by Maoist propaganda, rousing, rhetorical speeches and an obedient audience with glazed eyes. We arrive at the grounds quite late in the evening. A temporary monument of bamboo scaffolding wrapped in red cloth has been erected. On top, above the hammer and sickle of the Maoist Party, is the bow and arrow of the Janatana Sarkar, wrapped in silver foil. Appropriate, the hierarchy. The stage is huge, also temporary, on a sturdy scaffolding covered by a thick layer of mud

The Maoists are not the only ones who seek to depose the Indian State. It's already been deposed several times, by Hindu fundamentalism and economic totalitarianism.

plaster. Already there are small fires scattered around the ground, people have begun to arrive and are cooking their evening meal. They're only silhouettes in the dark. We thread our way through them (*lalsalaam, lalsalaam, lalsalaam*) and keep going for about fifteen minutes until we re-enter the forest.

At our new campsite we have to fall in again. Another roll call. And then instructions about sentry positions and 'firing arcs'—decisions about who will cover which area in the event of a police attack. RV points are fixed again.

An advance party has arrived and cooked dinner already. For dessert Kamla brings me a wild guava that she has plucked on the walk and squirrelled away for me.

From dawn there is the sense of more and more people gathering for the day's celebration. There's a buzz of excitement building up. People who haven't seen each other in a long time meet again. We can hear the sound of mikes being tested. Flags, banners, posters, buntings are going up. A poster with the pictures of the five people who were killed in Ongnaar the day we arrived has appeared.

I'm drinking tea with Comrade Narmada, Comrade Maase and Comrade Roopi. Comrade Narmada talks about the many years she worked in Gadchiroli before becoming the DK head of the Krantikari Adivasi

Mahila Sangathan. Roopi and Maase have been urban activists in Andhra Pradesh and tell me about the long years of struggle of women *within* the Party, not just for their rights, but also to make the Party see that equality between men and women is central to a dream of a just society. We talk about the '70s and the stories of women within the Naxalite movement who were disillusioned by male comrades who thought themselves great revolutionaries but were hobbled by the same old patriarchy, the same old chauvinism. Maase says things have changed a lot since then, though they still have a long way to go. (The Party's Politburo has no women yet. The Central Committee had Anuradha Gandhy— who died of cerebral malaria last year—and Sheela, an adivasi comrade who is now in jail.)

Around noon another PLGA contingent arrives. This one is headed by a tall, lithe, boyish-looking man. This comrade has two names—Sukhdev and Gudsa Usendi—neither of which is his. Sukhdev is the name of a very beloved comrade who was martyred. (In this war only the dead are safe enough to use their real names.) As for Gudsa Usendi, many comrades have been Gudsa Usendi at one point or another. (A few months ago it was Comrade Raju.) Gudsa Usendi is the name of the Party's spokesperson for Dandakaranya. So even though Sukhdev spends the rest of the trip with me, I have no idea how I'd ever find him again. I'd recognize his laugh anywhere though. He came to DK in '88 he says, when the PWG decided to send one third of its forces from north Telangana into DK. He's nicely dressed, in 'civil' (Gondi for 'civilian clothes') as opposed to 'dress' (the Maoist 'uniform'), and could pass off as a young executive. I ask him why no uniform.

He says he's been travelling and has just come back from the Keshkal Ghats near Kanker. There are reports of bauxite deposits—three million tonnes—that a company called Vedanta has its eye on.

Bingo. Ten on ten for instinct.

Sukhdev says he went there to measure the people's temperature. To see if they were prepared to fight. 'They want squads now. And guns.' He throws his head back and roars with laughter. 'I told them it's not so easy, bhai.' From the stray wisps of conversation and the ease with which he carries his AK-47, I can tell he's also high up and hands-on PLGA.

Jungle post arrives. There's a biscuit for me! It's from Comrade Venu. On a tiny piece of paper, folded and refolded, he has written down the lyrics of a song he promised he would send me. Comrade Narmada smiles when she reads them. She knows this story. It goes back to the '80s, around the time when people first began to trust the Party and come to it with their problems—their 'inner contradictions' as Comrade Venu put it. Women were among the first to come. One evening an old lady sitting by the fire got up and sang a song for the Dada log. She was a Maadiya, among whom it was customary for women to remove their blouses and remain bare-breasted after they were married.

Jumper polo intor Dada, Dakoniley
Taane tasom intor Dada, Dakoniley
Bata papam kittom Dada, Dakoniley
Duniya kadile maata Dada, Dakoniley
They say we cannot keep our blouses, Dada,
    Dakoniley
They make us take them off Dada,
In what way have we sinned Dada,
The world has changed, has it not, Dada,
Aatum hatteke Dada, Dakoniley
Aada nanga dantom Dada, Dakoniley
Id pisval manni Dada, Dakoniley
Mava koyaturku vehat Dada, Dakoniley
But when we go to market Dada,
We have to go half-naked Dada,
We don't want this life Dada,
Tell our ancestors this Dada.

This was the first women's issue the Party decided to campaign against. It had to be handled delicately, with surgical tools. In 1986 it set up the Adivasi Mahila Sangathan (AMS), which then evolved into the Krantikari Adivasi Mahila Sangathan and now has 90,000 enrolled members. It could well be the largest women's organization in the country. (They're all Maoists by the way, all 90,000 of them. Are they going to be 'wiped out'? And what about the 10,000 members of CNM? Them too?) The KAMS campaigns against the adivasi traditions of forced marriage and abduction. Against the custom of making menstruating women live outside the village in a hut in the forest. Against bigamy and domestic violence. It hasn't won all its battles, but then which feminists have? For instance, in Dandakaranya, even today, women are not allowed to sow seeds. In Party meetings men agree that this is unfair and ought to be done away with. But in practice, they simply don't allow it. So the Party decided that women would sow seeds on common lands, which belongs to the Janatana Sarkar. On that land they sow seeds, grow vegetables and build check dams. A half-victory, not a whole one.

As police repression has grown in Bastar, the women of KAMS have become a formidable force and rally in their hundreds, sometimes thousands, to physically confront the police. The very fact that the KAMS exists has radically changed traditional attitudes and eased many of the traditional forms of discrimination against women. For many young women, joining the Party, in particular the PLGA, became a way of escaping the suffocation of their own society. Comrade Sushila, a senior office-bearer of KAMS, talks about the Salwa Judum's rage against KAMS women. She says one of their slogans was *Hum do bibi layenge! Layenge!* (We will have two wives! We will!) A lot of the rape and bestial sexual mutilation was directed at members of the KAMS. Many young women who witnessed the savagery then joined the PLGA and women now make up 45 per cent of its cadre. Comrade Narmada sends for some of them and they join us in a while.

Comrade Rinki has very short hair. A bob cut as they say in Gondi. It's brave of her, because here 'bob cut' means 'Maoist'. For the police that's more than enough evidence to warrant summary execution. Comrade Rinki's village, Korma, was attacked by the Naga Battalion and the Salwa Judum in 2005. At that time Rinki was part of the village militia. So were her friends Lukki and Sukki, who were also members of the KAMS. After burning the village, the Naga Battalion caught Lukki and Sukki and one other girl, gang-raped them and killed them. 'They raped them on the grass,' Rinki says, 'but after it was over there was no grass left.' It's been years now, the Naga

GUNDADHUR LED THE BHUMKAL UPRISING IN 1910

Bhumkal, Comrade Raju says, means earthquake. He says people will walk for days together to come for the celebration. The forest must be full of people on the move. There are celebrations in all the Dandakaranya divisions.

ACTORS OF THE CHETNA
NATYA MANCH
'There are 10,000 members in
CNM now,' Comrade Leng,
head of the CNM, told me.
'We have 500 songs, in Hindi,
Gondi, Chhattisgarhi and Halbi.
We have printed a book with
140 of our songs. Everybody
writes songs.'

Battalion has gone, but the police still come. 'They come whenever they need women, or chickens.'

Ajitha has a bob-cut too. The Judum came to Korseel, her village, and killed three people by drowning them in a stream. Ajitha was with the militia, and followed the Judum at a distance to a place close to the village called Paral Nar Todak. She watched them rape six women and shoot a man in his throat.

Comrade Laxmi, who has a long, thick plait, tells me she watched the Judum burn thirty houses in her village, Jojor. 'We had no weapons then,' she says. 'We could do nothing but watch.' She joined the PLGA soon after. Laxmi was one of the 150 guerrillas who walked through the jungle for three and a half months in 2008, to Nayagarh in Orissa, to raid a police armoury from where they captured 1200 rifles and 200,000 rounds of ammunition.

Comrade Sumitra joined the PLGA in 2004, before the Salwa Judum began its rampage. She joined, she says, because she wanted to escape from home. 'Women are controlled in every way,' she told me. 'In our village girls were not allowed to climb trees; if they did, they would have to pay a fine of ₹500 or a hen. If a man hits a woman and she hits him back she has to give the village a goat. Men go off to the hills for months together to hunt. Women are not allowed to go near the kill, the best part of the meat goes to men. Women are not allowed to eat eggs.'

Good reason to join a guerrilla army?

Sumitra tells the story of two of her friends, Telam Parvati and Kamla, who worked with KAMS. Telam Parvati was from Pollevaya village in west Bastar. Like everyone else from there, she too watched the Salwa Judum burn her village. She then joined the PLGA and went to work in the Keshkal Ghats. In 2009 she and Kamla had just finished organizing the 8 March Women's Day celebrations in the area. They were together in a little hut just outside a village called Vadgo. The police surrounded the hut at night and began to fire. Kamla fired back, but she was killed. Parvati escaped, but was found and killed the next day.

That's what happened last year on Women's Day. And here's a press report from a national newspaper about Women's Day this year.

Bastar rebels bat for women's rights
Sahar Khan, *Mail Today*, Raipur, March 7, 2010
The government may have pulled out all stops to combat the Maoist

They even have a Gandhian approach to sabotage; before a police vehicle is burnt, it is stripped down. The steering wheel is straightened out and made into a bharmaar barrel, the rexine upholstery stripped and used for ammunition pouches... (And backpacks).

menace in the country. But a section of rebels in Chhattisgarh has more pressing matters in hand than survival. With International Women's Day around the corner, Maoists in the Bastar region of the state have called for week-long 'celebrations' to advocate women's rights. Posters were also put up in Bijapur, a part of Bastar district. The call by the self-styled champions of women's rights has left the state police astonished. Inspector-general (IG) of Bastar T. J. Longkumer said, 'I have never seen such an appeal from the Naxalites, who believe only in violence and bloodshed.'

And then the report goes on to say:

'I think the Maoists are trying to counter our highly successful Jan Jagran Abhiyaan (mass awareness campaign). We started the ongoing campaign with an aim to win popular support for Operation Green Hunt, which was launched by the police to root out Left-wing extremists,' the IG said.

This cocktail of malice and ignorance is not unusual. Gudsa Usendi, chronicler of the Party's present, knows more about this than most people. His little computer and MP3 recorder are full of press statements, denials, corrections, Party literature, lists of the dead, TV clips and audio and video material. 'The worst thing about being Gudsa Usendi,' he says, 'is issuing clarifications that are never published. We could bring out a thick book of our unpublished clarifications, about the lies they tell about us.' He speaks without a trace of indignation, in fact with some amusement.

'What's the most ridiculous charge you've had to deny?'

He thinks back. 'In 2007, we had to issue a statement saying *"Nahi bhai, humney gai ko hathode say nahin mara"* [No, brother, we did not kill cows with hammers]. In 2007 the Raman Singh government announced a Gai Yojana [cow scheme], an election promise, a cow for every adivasi. One day the TV channels and newspapers reported that Naxalites had attacked a herd of cows and bludgeoned them to death—with hammers—because they were anti-Hindu, anti-BJP. You can imagine what happened. We issued a denial. Hardly anybody carried it. Later it turned out that the man who had been given the cows to distribute was a rogue. He sold them and said we had ambushed him and killed the cows.'

And the most serious?

'Oh there are dozens, they're running a campaign after all. When the Salwa Judum was first announced in Ambeli they first attacked our village-level activists whom they had invited for the meeting, they beat them up and handed them over to the police. Then all of them, SPOs, the Naga Battalion, police, moved towards

Tadimendri. There our local guerrilla squad comrades fired in the air and drove them away. No one was hurt, but Annie Zaidi of *Frontline* said, and these are her words, "At a meeting at Talmendra, attended by more than 10,000 people, naxalites allegedly opened fire and killed hundreds of people."[7] That same day the Judum went to Kotrapal—you must have heard about Kotrapal? It's a famous village; it has been burnt twenty-two times for refusing to surrender. When they reached Kotrapal, our militia was waiting for it. They had prepared an ambush. Three Salwa Judum goons were killed. The militia captured twelve, the rest ran away. But the newspapers reported that the Naxalites had massacred dozens of poor adivasis. Even K. Balagopal, the human rights activist, who is usually meticulous about facts, put the figure at eighteen in a press release by the Human Rights Forum. We sent a clarification. Nobody published it. Later, in his book, Balagopal acknowledged his mistake.... But who noticed?"[8]

I asked what happened to the twelve people who were captured.

'The Area Committee called a Jan Adalat [People's Court]. Four thousand people attended it. They listened to the whole story. Two were sentenced to death. Of them one escaped. The rest were warned and let off. The people decided. Even with informers—which is becoming a huge problem nowadays—people listen to the case, the stories, the confessions and say, *"Iska hum risk nahin le sakte"* [We're not prepared to take the risk] or, *"Iska risk hum lenge"* [We are prepared to take the risk]. The press always reports about informers who are killed. Never about the many that are let *off.* Never about the people whom these informers have had killed. So everybody thinks it is some bloodthirsty procedure in which everybody is always killed. It's not about revenge, it's about survival and saving future lives.... Of course there are problems, we've made terrible mistakes, we have even killed the wrong people in our ambushes, thinking they were policemen, but it is not the way it's portrayed in the media.'

The dreaded 'People's Courts'. How can we accept them? Or approve this form of rude justice? On the other hand, what about 'encounters' fake and otherwise—the worst form of summary justice—that get policemen and soldiers bravery medals, cash awards and out-of-turn promotions from the Indian government? The more they kill, the more they are rewarded. 'Bravehearts' they are called, the 'encounter specialists'. 'Anti-nationals' we are called, those of us who dare to question them. And what about the Supreme Court that brazenly admitted it did not have enough evidence to sentence Mohammed Afzal (accused in the December 2001 Parliament Attack)

MILITIA AT BHUMKAL CELEBRATIONS

In this tranquil-looking forest, life seems completely militarized now. People know words like Cordon and Search, Firing, Advance, Retreat, Down, Action! To harvest their crops they need the PLGA to do a sentry patrol. Going to the market is a military operation.

**CURTAIN-RAISER AT THE
BHUMKAL CELEBRATION**
I'm not sure whether I'm
looking forward to the Bhumkal
celebrations. I fear I'll see
traditional tribal dances stiffened
by Maoist propaganda, rousing,
rhetorical speeches and an
obedient audience with
glazed eyes.

to death, but did so anyway, because 'the collective conscience of the society will only be satisfied if capital punishment is awarded to the offender'.[9]

At least in the case of the Kotrapal Jan Adalat, the Collective was physically present to make its own decision. It wasn't made by judges who had lost touch with ordinary life a long time ago, but still presumed to speak on behalf of an absent Collective.

What should the people of Kotrapal have done? I wonder. Sent for the police?

~

The sound of drums has become really loud. It's Bhumkal time. We walk to the grounds. I can hardly believe my eyes. There is a sea of people, the most wild, beautiful people, dressed in the most wild, beautiful ways. The men seem to have paid much more attention to themselves than the women. They have feathered headgear and painted tattoos on their faces. Many have eye make-up and white, powdered faces. There's lots of militia, girls in saris of breathtaking colours with rifles slung carelessly over their shoulders. There are old people, children, and red buntings arc across the sky. The sun is sharp and high. Comrade Leng speaks. And several office-bearers of the various Janatana Sarkars. Comrade Niti, an extraordinary woman who has been with the Party since 1997, is such a threat to the nation that in January 2007 more than 700 policemen surrounded Innar village because they heard she was there. Comrade Niti is considered so dangerous, and is being hunted with such desperation, not because she has led many ambushes (which she has), but because she is an adivasi woman who is loved in the village and is a real inspiration to young people. She speaks with her AK on her shoulder. (It's a gun with a story. Almost everyone's gun has a story: who it was snatched from, how and by whom.)

A CNM troupe performs a play about the Bhumkal uprising. The evil white colonizers wear hats and golden straw for hair, and bully and beat adivasis to pulp—causing endless delight in the audience. Another troupe from south Gangalaur performs a play called *Nitir Judum Pito* (Story of the Blood Hunt). Joori translates for me. It's the story of two old people who go looking for their daughter's village. As they walk through the forest, they get lost because everything is burnt and unrecognizable. The Salwa Judum has even burned the drums and the musical instruments. There are no ashes because it has been raining. They cannot find their daughter. In their sorrow the old couple starts to sing and, hearing them, the voice of their daughter sings back to them from the ruins: The sound of our village has been silenced, she sings. There's no more pounding of rice, no more laughter by the well. No more birds, no more bleating goats. The taut string of our happiness has been snapped.

Her father sings back: My beautiful daughter, don't cry today. Everyone who is born must die. These trees around us will fall, flowers will bloom and fade, one day this world will grow old. But who are we dying for? One day our looters will learn, one day Truth will prevail, but our people will never forget you, not for thousands of years.

A few more speeches. Then the drumming and the dancing begin. Each Janatana Sarkar has its own troupe. Each troupe has prepared its own dance. They arrive one by one, with huge drums and they dance wild stories. The only character every troupe has in common is Bad Mining Man, with a helmet and dark glasses, and usually smoking a cigarette. There's nothing stiff or mechanical about their dancing. As they dance, the dust rises. The sound of drums becomes deafening. Gradually, the crowd begins to sway. And then it begins to dance. They dance in little lines of six or seven, men and women separate, with their arms around each other's waists. Thousands of people. This is what they've come for. For this. Happiness is taken very seriously here, in the Dandakaranya forest. People will walk for miles, for days together to feast and sing, to put feathers in their turbans and flowers in their hair, to put their arms around each other and drink mahua and dance through the night. No one sings or dances alone. This, more than anything else, signals their defiance towards a civilization that seeks to annihilate them.

I can't believe all this is happening right under the noses of the police. Right in the midst of Operation Green Hunt.

At first the PLGA comrades watch the dancers, standing aside with their guns. But then, one by one, like ducks who cannot bear to stand on the shore and watch other ducks swim, they move in and begin to dance too. Soon there are lines of olive-green dancers, swirling with all the other colours. And then, as sisters and brothers and parents and children and friends who haven't met for months, years sometimes, encounter each other, the lines break up and re-form and the olive green is distributed among the swirling saris and flowers and drums and turbans. It surely is a People's Army. For now, at least. And what Chairman Mao said about the guerrillas being the fish, and people being the water they swim in, is, at this moment, literally true.

Chairman Mao. He's here too. A little lonely, perhaps, but present. There's a photograph of him, up on a red cloth screen. Marx too. And Charu Mazumdar, the founder and chief theoretician of the Naxalite

A TRANSIENT MEMORIAL
TO THE MARTYRS
A few more speeches.
Then the drumming and the
dancing begin. Each Janatana
Sarkar has its own troupe.
Each troupe has prepared
its own dance.

BHUMKAL BEGINS

Happiness is taken very seriously here, in the Dandakaranya forest. People will walk for miles, for days together to feast and sing, to put feathers in their turbans and flowers in their hair, to put their arms around each other and drink mahua and dance through the night. No one sings or dances alone. This, more than anything else, signals their defiance towards a civilization that seeks to annihilate them.

movement. His abrasive rhetoric fetishizes violence, blood and martyrdom, and often employs a language so coarse as to be almost genocidal. Standing here, on Bhumkal day, I can't help thinking that his analysis, so vital to the structure of this revolution, is so removed from its emotion and texture. 'Only by waging class struggle—the battle of annihilation—the new man will be created, the new man who will defy death and will be free from all thoughts of self-interest'[10]—could he have imagined that this ancient people, dancing into the night, would be the ones on whose shoulders his dreams would come to rest?

It's a great disservice to everything that is happening here that the only thing that seems to make it to the outside world is the stiff, unbending rhetoric of the ideologues of a party that has evolved from a problematic past. When Charu Mazumdar famously said, 'China's chairman is our chairman and China's path is our path,' he was prepared to extend it to the point where the Naxalites remained silent while General Yahya Khan committed genocide in East Pakistan (Bangladesh). Because, at the time, China was an ally of Pakistan. There was silence too over the Khmer Rouge and its killing fields in Cambodia. There was silence over the egregious excesses of the Chinese and Russian revolutions. Silence over Tibet. Within the Naxalite movement too, there have been violent excesses and it's impossible to defend much of what they've done. But can anything they have done compare with the sordid achievements of the Congress and the BJP in Punjab, Kashmir, Delhi, Mumbai, Gujarat.... And yet, despite these terrifying contradictions, Charu Mazumdar, in much of what he wrote and said, was a man with a political vision for India that cannot be dismissed lightly. The party he founded (and its many splinter groups) has kept the dream of revolution *real* and present in India. Imagine a society without that dream. For that alone we cannot judge him too harshly. Especially not while we swaddle ourselves with Gandhi's pious humbug about the superiority of 'the non-violent way' and his notion of Trusteeship: 'The rich man will be left in possession of his wealth, of which he will use what he reasonably requires for his personal needs and will act as a trustee for the remainder to be used for the good of society.'

How strange it is though, that the contemporary tsars of the Indian Establishment—the State that crushed the Naxalites so mercilessly—should now be saying what Charu Mazumdar said so long ago: China's Path is Our Path.

Upside Down. Inside Out.

China's Path has changed. China is on its way to becoming an imperial power now, fuelled by the raw materials of other countries. But the Party is still right, only, the Party has changed its mind.

When the Party is a suitor (as it is now in Dandakaranya), wooing the people, attentive to their every need, then it genuinely is a People's Party, its army genuinely a People's Army. But after the Revolution, how easily this love affair can turn into a bitter marriage. How easily the People's Army can turn upon the people. Today in Dandakaranya, the Party wants to keep the bauxite in the mountain. Tomorrow will it change its mind? But can we, should we, let apprehensions about the future immobilize us in the present?

The dancing will go on all night. I walk back to the camp. Maase is there, awake. We chat late into the night. I give her my copy of Neruda's *Captain's Verses*. (I brought it along, just in case.) She asks again and again, 'What do they think of us outside? What do students say? Tell me about the women's movement, what are the big issues now?' She asks about me, my writing. I try and give her an honest account of my chaos. Then she starts to talk about herself, how she joined the Party. She tells me that her partner was killed last May, in a fake encounter. He was arrested in Nashik, and taken to Warangal to be killed. 'They must have tortured him badly.' She was on her way to meet him when she heard he had been arrested. She's been in the forest ever since. After a long silence she tells me she was married once before, years ago. 'He was killed in an encounter too,' she says, and adds with heartbreaking precision, 'but in a real one.'

I lie awake on my jhilli, thinking of Maase's protracted sadness, listening to the drums and the sounds of protracted happiness from the grounds, and thinking about Charu Mazumdar's idea of protracted war, the central precept of the Maoist Party. This is what makes people think the Maoists' offer to enter 'peace talks' is a hoax, a ploy to get breathing space to regroup, rearm themselves and go back to waging protracted war. What is protracted war? Is it a terrible thing in itself, or does it depend on the nature of the war? What if the people here in Dandakaranya had not waged their protracted war for the last thirty years, where would they be now?

And are the Maoists the only ones who believe in protracted war? Almost from the moment India became a sovereign nation it turned into a colonial power, annexing territory, waging war. It has never hesitated to use military interventions to address political problems— Kashmir, Hyderabad, Goa, Nagaland, Manipur, Telangana, Assam, Punjab, the Naxalite uprising in West Bengal, Bihar, Andhra Pradesh and now across the tribal areas of central India. Tens of thousands have been killed with impunity, hundreds of thousands tortured. All of this behind the benign mask of democracy. Who have these wars been waged against? Muslims, Christians, Sikhs, Communists, Tribals and, most of all, against the poor, for the most part Dalits, who dare to question their lot instead of accepting the crumbs that are flung at them. It's hard not to see the Indian State as an essentially upper-caste Hindu State (regardless of which party is in power) which harbours a reflexive hostility towards the 'other'. One that in true colonial fashion sends the Nagas and Mizos to fight in Chhattisgarh, Sikhs to Kashmir, Kashmiris to Orissa, Tamilians to Assam and so on. If this isn't protracted war, what is?

Unpleasant thoughts on a lovely, starry night. Sukhdev is smiling to himself, his face lit by his computer screen. He's a crazy workaholic. I ask him what's funny. 'I was thinking about the journalists who came last year for the Bhumkal celebrations. They came for a day or two. One posed with my AK, had himself photographed and then went back and called us Killing Machines or something.'

~

The dancing hasn't stopped and it's daybreak. The lines are still going, hundreds of young people still dancing. 'They won't stop,' Comrade Raju says, 'not until we start packing up.'

On the grounds I run into Comrade Doctor. He's

been running a little medical camp on the edge of the dance floor. I want to kiss his fat cheeks. Why can't he be at least thirty people instead of just one? Why can't he be one thousand people? I ask him what it's looking like, the health of Dandakaranya. His reply makes my blood run cold. Most of the people he has seen, he says, including those in the PLGA, have a haemoglobin count that's far, far below the standard for Indian women, eleven. There's TB caused by more than two years of chronic anaemia. Young children suffer from Protein Energy Malnutrition Grade II, in medical terminology called Kwashiorkor. (I looked it up later. It's a word derived from the Ga language of Coastal Ghana and means 'the sickness a baby gets when the new baby comes'. Basically the old baby stops getting mother's milk, and there's not enough food to provide it nutrition.) 'It's an epidemic here, like in Biafra,' Comrade Doctor says. 'I have worked in villages before, but I've never seen anything like this.'

Apart from this, there's malaria, osteoporosis, tapeworm, severe ear and tooth infections and primary amenorrhoea—which is when malnutrition during puberty causes a woman's menstrual cycle to disappear, or never appear in the first place.

'There are no clinics in this forest apart from one or two in Gadchiroli. No doctors. No medicines.'

He's off now, with his little team, on an eight-day

THE DANCING WILL GO ON ALL NIGHT

At first the PLGA comrades watch the dancers, standing aside with their guns. But then, one by one, like ducks who cannot bear to stand on the shore and watch other ducks swim, they move in and begin to dance too. Soon there are lines of olive-green dancers, swirling with all the other colours.

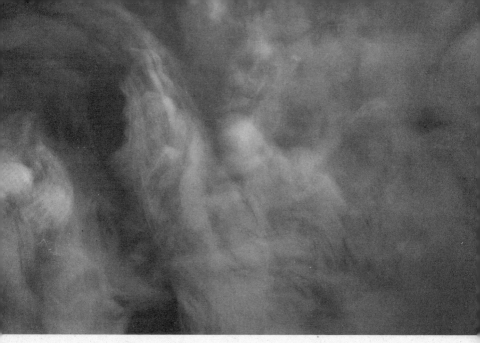

THE DANCING HASN'T STOPPED AND IT'S DAYBREAK

As sisters and brothers and
parents and children and friends
who haven't met for months,
years sometimes, encounter each
other, the lines break up and
re-form and the olive green is
distributed among the swirling
saris and flowers and drums
and turbans.

trek to Abujhmad. He's in 'dress' too, Comrade Doctor. So if they find him they'll kill him.

Comrade Raju says that it isn't safe for us to continue to camp here. We have to move. Leaving Bhumkal involves a lot of goodbyes spread over time.

Lal lal salaam, lal lal salaam,

Jaane vaaley saathiyon ko lal lal salaam,

(Red Salute to departing comrades)

Phir milenge, phir milenge

Dandakaranya jungle mein phir milenge

(We'll meet again, some day, in the Dandakaranya forest.)

It's never taken lightly, the ceremony of arrival and departure, because everybody knows that when they say 'we'll meet again' they actually mean 'we may never meet again'. Comrade Narmada, Comrade Maase and Comrade Roopi are going separate ways. Will I ever see them again?

So once again, we walk. It's becoming hotter every day. Kamla picks the first fruit of the tendu for me. It tastes like chikoo. I've become a tamarind fiend. This time we camp near a stream. Women and men take turns to bathe in batches. In the evening Comrade Raju receives a whole packet of 'biscuits'.

News:

60 people arrested in Manpur Division at the end of

January 2010 have not yet been produced in Court.

Huge contingents of police have arrived in south Bastar. Indiscriminate attacks are on.

On 8 November 2009, in Kachlaram village, Bijapur jila, Dirko Madka (60) and Kovasi Suklu (68) were killed.

On 24 November Madavi Baman (15) was killed in Pangodi village.

On 3 December Madavi Budram from Korenjad also killed.

On 11 December Gumiapal village, Darba division, 7 people killed (names yet to come).

On 15 December Kotrapal village, Veko Sombar and Madavi Matti (both with KAMS) killed.

On 30 December Vechapal village Poonem Pandu and Poonem Motu (father and son) killed.

In January 2010 (date unknown) Head of the Janatana Sarkar in Kaika village, Gangalaur killed.

On 9 January, 4 people killed in Surpangooden village, Jagargonda area.

A runner, with 'biscuits'. Handwritten notes on sheets of paper, folded and stapled into little squares. News from everywhere. The police have killed five people in Ongnaar village …

On 10 January, 3 people killed in Pullem Pulladi village (no names yet).

On 25 January, 7 people killed in Takilod village, Indravati area.

On February 10 (Bhumkal Day) Kumli raped and killed in Dumnaar village, Abujhmad. She was from a village called Paiver.

2000 troops of the ITBP are camped in the Rajnandgaon forests.

5000 additional BSF troops have arrived in Kanker.

And then:

PLGA quota filled.

Some dated newspapers have arrived too. There's a lot of press about Naxalites. One screaming headline sums up the political climate perfectly: *'Khadedo, maaro, samarpan karao'* (Eliminate, kill, make them surrender). Below that: *'Varta ke liye loktantra ka dwar khula hai'* (Democracy's door is always open for talks). A second says the Maoists are growing cannabis to make money. The third has an editorial saying that the area we've camped in and are walking through is entirely under police control.

The young communists take the clips away to practise their reading. They walk around the camp reading the anti-Maoist articles loudly in radio-announcer voices.

~

New day. New place. We're camped on the outskirts of Usir village, under huge mahua trees. The mahua has just begun to flower and is dropping its pale-green blossoms like jewels on the forest floor. The air is suffused with its slightly heady smell. We're waiting for the children from the Bhatpal school, which was closed down after the Ongnaar encounter. It's been turned into a police camp. The children have been sent home. This is also true of the schools in Nelwad, Moonjmetta, Edka, Vedomakot and Dhanora.

The Bhatpal school children don't show up.

Comrade Niti (Most Wanted) and Comrade Vinod lead us on a long walk to see the series of water-harvesting structures and irrigation ponds that have been built by the local Janatana Sarkar. Comrade Niti talks about the range of agricultural problems they have to deal with. Only 2 per cent of the land is irrigated. In Abujhmad, ploughing was unheard of until ten years ago. In Gadchiroli, on the other hand, hybrid seeds and chemical pesticides are edging their way in. 'We need urgent help in the agriculture department,' Comrade Vinod says. 'We need people who know about seeds, organic pesticides, permaculture. With a little help we could do a lot.'

Comrade Ramu is the farmer in charge of the Janatana Sarkar area. He proudly shows us around the fields, where they grow rice, brinjal, gongura, onion, kohlrabi. Then, with equal pride, he shows us a huge, but bone-dry, irrigation pond. What's this? 'This one doesn't even have water during the rainy season. It's dug in the wrong place,' he says, a smile wrapped around his face. 'It's not ours, it was dug by the Looti Sarkar' (the Government that Loots). There are two parallel systems of government here, Janatana Sarkar and Looti Sarkar.

I think of what Comrade Venu said to me: They want to crush us, not only because of the minerals, but because we are offering the world an alternative model.

It's not an Alternative yet, this idea of Gram Swaraj with a Gun. There is too much hunger, too much sickness here. But it has certainly created the possibilities for an alternative. Not for the whole world, not for Alaska, or New Delhi, nor even perhaps for the whole of Chhattisgarh, but for itself. For Dandakaranya. It's the world's best-kept secret. It has laid the foundations for an alternative to its own annihilation. It has defied history. Against the greatest odds it has forged a blueprint for its own survival. It needs help and imagination, it needs doctors, teachers, farmers.

It does not need war.

But if war is all it gets, it will fight back.

~

Over the next few days I meet women who work with KAMS, various office-bearers of the Janatana Sarkars, members of the Dandakaranya Adivasi Kisan Mazdoor Sangathan (DAKMS), the families of people who had been killed, and just ordinary people trying to cope with life in these terrifying times.

I met three sisters, Sukhiari, Sukdai and Sukkali, not young, perhaps in their forties, from Narainpur district. They have been in KAMS for twelve years. The villagers depend on them to deal with the police. 'The police come in groups of two to three hundred. They steal everything, jewellery, chickens, pigs, pots and pans, bows and arrows,' Sukkali says, 'they won't even leave a knife.' Her house in Innar has been burned twice, once by the Naga Battalion and once by the CRPF. Sukhiari has been arrested and jailed in Jagdalpur for seven months. 'Once they took away the whole village, saying the men were all Naxals.' Sukhiari followed with all the women and children. They surrounded the police station and refused to leave until the men were freed. 'Whenever they take someone away,' Sukdai says, 'you have to go immediately and snatch them back. Before they write any report. Once they write in their book, it becomes very difficult.'

Sukhiari, who as a child was abducted and forcibly married to an older man (she ran away and went to live with her sister), now organizes mass rallies, speaks at meetings. The men depend on her for protection. I asked her what the Party means to her. '*Naxalvaad ka matlab humaara parivaar* [Naxalism means our family]. When we hear of an attack, it is like our family has been hurt,' Sukhiari said.

I asked her if she knew who Mao was. She smiled shyly. 'He was a leader. We're working for his vision.'

I met Comrade Somari Gawde. Twenty years old, and she has already served a two-year jail sentence in Jagdalpur. She was in Innar village on 8 January 2007, the day that 740 policemen laid a cordon around it because they had information that Comrade Niti was there. (She was, but had left by the time they arrived.) But the village militia, of which Somari was a member, was still there. The police opened fire at dawn. They killed two boys, Suklal Gawde and Kachroo Gota. Then they caught three others, two boys, Dusri Salam and Ranai, and Somari. Dusri and Ranai were tied up and shot. Somari was beaten within an inch of her life. The police got a tractor with a trailer and loaded the dead bodies into it. Somari was made to sit with the dead bodies and taken to Narainpur.

I met Chamri, mother of Comrade Dilip who was

shot on 6 July 2009. She says that, after they killed him, the police tied her son's body to a pole, like an animal, and carried it with them. (They need to produce bodies to get their cash rewards, before someone else muscles in on the kill.) Chamri ran behind them all the way to the police station. By the time they reached their destination, the body did not have a scrap of clothing on it. On the way, Chamri says, they left the body by the roadside while they stopped at a dhaba to have tea and biscuits. (Which they did not pay for.) Picture this mother for a moment, following her son's corpse through the forest,

SUKHIARI, SUKDAI AND SUKKALI In 1986 the Party set up the Adivasi Mahila Sangathan, which evolved into the Krantikari Adivasi Mahila Sangathan and now has 90,000 members. Are they all going to be 'wiped out'?

stopping at a distance to wait for his murderers to finish their tea. They did not let her have her son's body back so she could give him a proper funeral. They only let her throw a fistful of earth in the pit in which they buried the others they had killed that day. Chamri says she wants revenge. *Badla ku badla*. Revenge. Blood for blood.

I met the elected members of the Marskola Janatana Sarkar that administers six villages. They described a police raid: They come at night, three hundred, four hundred, sometimes a thousand of them. They lay a cordon around a village and lie in wait. At dawn they catch the first people who go out to the fields and use them as human shields to enter the village, to show them where the booby traps are. ('Booby traps', like 'RV', has become a Gondi word. Everybody always smiles when they say it or hear it. The forest is full of booby traps, real and fake. Even the PLGA needs to be guided past villages.) Once the police enter the village they loot and steal and burn houses. They come with dogs. The dogs catch those who try to run. They chase chickens and pigs and the police kill them and take them away in sacks. SPOs come along with the police. They're the ones who know where people hide their money and jewellery. They catch people and take them away. And extract money before they release them. They always carry some extra Naxal 'dresses' with them in case they find someone to kill. They get money for killing Naxals, so they manufacture some. Villagers are too frightened to stay at home.

In this tranquil-looking forest, life seems completely militarized now. People know words like Cordon and Search, Firing, Advance, Retreat, Down, Action! To harvest their crops they need the PLGA to do a sentry patrol. Going to the market is a military operation. The markets are full of mukhbirs (informers) who the police have lured from their villages with money (₹1500 a month). I'm told there's a mukhbir mohallah—informers' colony—in Narainpur where at least 400 mukhbirs stay. The men can't go to market any more. The women go, but they're watched closely. If they buy even a little extra, the police accuse them of buying it for Naxals. Chemists have instructions not to let people buy medicines except in very small quantities. Low-price rations from the public distribution system, sugar, rice, kerosene, are warehoused in or near police stations making it impossible for most people to buy.

~

Article 2 of the United Nations Convention on the Prevention and Punishment of the Crime of Genocide defines it as:

Any of the following Acts committed with intent to destroy, in whole or part, a national, ethnic, racial, or religious group, as such: killing members of the group; causing serious bodily or mental harm to members of the group; deliberately inflicting on the group conditions of life calculated to bring about its physical destruction in whole or part; imposing measures intended to prevent births within the group; [or] forcibly transferring children of the group to another group.

~

All the walking seems to have finally got to me. I'm tired. Kamla gets me a pot of hot water. I bathe behind a tree in the dark. But I can't eat dinner and crawl into my bag to sleep. Comrade Raju announces that we have to move. This happens frequently, of course, but tonight it's hard. We have been camped in an open meadow. We'd heard shelling in the distance. There are 104 of us. Once again, single file through the night. Crickets. The smell of something like lavender. It must have been past eleven when we arrived at the place where we will spend the night. An outcrop of rocks. Formation. Roll call. Someone switches on the radio. BBC says there's been an attack on a camp of Eastern Frontier Rifles in Lalgarh, West Bengal. Sixty Maoists on motorcycles. Fourteen policemen killed. Ten missing.

Weapons snatched. There's a murmur of pleasure in the ranks. The Maoist leader Kishenji is being interviewed. When will you stop this violence and come for talks? When Operation Green Hunt is called off. Any time. Tell Chidambaram we will talk. Next question: It's dark now, you have laid landmines, reinforcements have been called in, will you attack them too? Kishenji: Yes of course; otherwise people will beat me. There's laughter in the ranks. Sukhdev the clarifier says, 'They always say landmines. We don't use landmines. We use IEDs [improvised explosive devices].'

Another luxury suite in the thousand-star hotel. I'm feeling ill. It starts to rain. There's a little giggling. Kamla throws a jhilli over me. What more do I need? Everyone else just rolls themselves into their jhillis.

By next morning the body count in Lalgarh has gone up to twenty-one, ten missing.

Comrade Raju is considerate this morning. We don't move till evening.

~

One night people are crowded like moths around a point of light. It's Comrade Sukhdev's tiny computer, powered by a solar panel, and they're watching *Mother India*, the barrels of their rifles silhouetted against the sky. Kamla doesn't seem interested. I asked her if she

139

likes watching movies. *'Nahi, didi. Sirf ambush ka video.'*
(No, didi. Only the videos of our ambushes.) Later I ask
Comrade Sukhdev about these ambush videos. Without
batting an eyelid, he plays one for me.

It starts with shots of Dandakaranya, rivers, waterfalls,
the close-up of a bare branch of a tree, a brainfever bird
calling. Then suddenly a comrade is wiring up an IED,
concealing it with dry leaves. A cavalcade of motorcycles
is blown up. There are mutilated bodies and burning
bikes. The weapons are being snatched. Three policemen,
looking shell-shocked, have been tied up.

Who's filming it? Who's directing operations? Who's
reassuring the captured cops that they will be released if
they surrender? (They were released, I confirmed later.)

I know that gentle, reassuring voice. It's Comrade Venu.

'It's the Kudur Ambush,' Comrade Sukhdev says.

He also has a video archive of burnt villages,
testimonies from eyewitnesses and relatives of the dead.
On the singed wall of a burnt house it says, 'Nagaaa! Born
to Kill!' There's footage of the little boy whose fingers
were chopped off to inaugurate the Bastar chapter of
Operation Green Hunt. (There's even a TV interview
with me. My study. My books. Strange.)

At night on the radio there's news of another Naxal
attack. This one in Jamui, Bihar. It says 125 Maoists
attacked a village and killed ten people belonging to the

Kora tribe in retaliation for giving police information that led to the death of six Maoists. Of course we know, the report may or may not be true. But if it is, this one's unforgiveable. Comrades Raju and Sukhdev look distinctly uncomfortable.

The news that has been coming from Jharkhand and Bihar is disturbing. The gruesome beheading of the policeman Francis Induvar is still fresh in everyone's mind. It's a reminder of how easily the discipline of armed struggle can dissolve into lumpen acts of criminalized violence, or into ugly wars of identity between castes and communities and religious groups. By institutionalizing injustice in the way that it does, the Indian State has turned this country into a tinderbox of massive unrest. The government is quite wrong if it thinks that by carrying out 'targeted assassinations' to render the CPI (Maoist) 'headless' it will end the violence. On the contrary, the violence will spread and intensify, and the government will have nobody to talk to.

~

On my last few days we meander through the lush Indravati valley. As we walk along a hillside, we see another line of people walking in the same direction, but on the other side of the river. I'm told they're on their way to an anti-dam meeting in Kudur village. They're over ground and unarmed. A local rally for the valley. I jumped ship and joined them.

The Bodhghat Dam will submerge the entire area that we have been walking in for days. All that forest, that history, those stories. More than a hundred villages. Is that the plan then? To drown people like rats, so that the integrated steel plant in Lohandiguda and the bauxite mine and aluminium refinery in the Keshkal Ghats can have the river?

At the meeting, people who have come from miles away say the same thing we've all heard for years. We will drown, but we won't move! They are thrilled that someone from Delhi is with them. I tell them Delhi is a cruel city that neither knows nor cares about them.

Only weeks before I came to Dandakaranya, I visited Gujarat. The Sardar Sarovar Dam has more or less reached its full height now. And almost every single thing the Narmada Bachao Andolan predicted would happen has happened. People who were displaced have not been rehabilitated, but that goes without saying. The canals have not been built. There's no money. So Narmada water is being diverted into the empty riverbed of the Sabarmati (which was dammed a long time ago). Most of the water is being guzzled by cities and big industry. The downstream effects—saltwater ingress into an estuary with no river—are becoming impossible to mitigate.

There was a time when believing that Big Dams were the 'temples of Modern India' was misguided, but perhaps understandable. But today, after all that has happened, and when we know all that we do, it has to be said that Big Dams are a crime against humanity.

The Bodhghat Dam was shelved in 1984 after local people protested. Who will stop it now? Who will prevent the foundation stone from being laid? Who will stop the Indravati from being stolen? Someone must.

~

The Bodhghat Dam will submerge the entire area that we have been walking in for days. All that land. All that forest, that history, those stories.

On the last night we camped at the base of the steep hill we would climb in the morning, to emerge on the road from where a motorcycle would pick me up. The forest has changed even since I first entered it. The chironjee, silk cotton and mango trees have begun to flower.

The villagers from Kudur send a huge pot of freshly caught fish to the camp. And a list for me, of seventy-one kinds of fruit, vegetables, pulses and insects they get from the forest and grow in their fields, along with the market price. It's just a list. But it's also a map of their world.

Jungle post arrives. Two biscuits for me. A poem and a pressed flower from Comrade Narmada. A lovely letter from Maase. (Who is she? Will I ever know?)

Comrade Sukhdev asks if he can download the music from my iPod into his computer. We listen to a recording of Iqbal Bano singing Faiz Ahmed Faiz's *'Hum dekhenge'* (We will witness the day) at the famous concert in Lahore at the height of the repression during the Zia-ul-Haq years.

> *Jab ahl-e-safa-Mardud-e-haram,*
> *Masnad pe bithaiye jayenge*
> When the heretics and the reviled,
> Will be seated on high
> *Sab taaj uchhale jayenge*
> *Sab takht giraye jayenge*
> All crowns will be snatched away
> All thrones toppled
> *Hum dekhenge*

Fifty thousand people in the audience in *that* Pakistan begin a defiant chant: *Inqilab Zindabad! Inqilab Zindabad!* All these years later, that chant reverberates around this forest. Long live the Revolution! Strange, the alliances that get made.

The home minister has been issuing veiled threats to those who 'erroneously offer intellectual and material support to the Maoists'. Does sharing Iqbal Bano qualify?

At dawn I say goodbye to Comrade Madhav and Joori, to young Mangtu and all the others. Comrade Chandu has gone to organize the bikes, and will come with me up to the main road. Comrade Raju isn't coming. (The climb would be hell on his knees.) Comrade Niti (Most Wanted), Comrade Sukhdev, Kamla and five others will take me up the hill. As we start walking, Niti and Sukhdev casually, but simultaneously, unclick the safety catches of their AKs. It's the first time I've seen them do that. We're approaching the 'Border'. 'Do you know what to do if we come under fire?' Sukhdev asks casually, as though it was the most natural thing in the world.

'Yes,' I said. 'Immediately declare an indefinite hunger-strike.'

He sat down on a rock and laughed. We climbed for about an hour. Just below the road, we sat in a rocky alcove, completely concealed, like an ambush party, listening for the sound of the bikes. When it comes, the farewell must be quick. *Lal Salaam, Comrades.*

When I looked back, they were still there. Waving. A little knot. People who live with their dreams, while the rest of the world lives with its nightmares. Every night I think of this journey. That night sky, those forest paths.

I see Comrade Kamla's heels in her scuffed chappals, lit by the light of my torch. I know she must be on the move. Marching, not just for herself, but to keep hope alive for us all.

March 2010

The law locks up the hapless felon
who steals the goose from off the common,
but lets the greater felon loose
who steals the common from the goose.

ANONYMOUS, ENGLAND, 1821[1]

In the early morning hours of 2 July 2010, in the remote forests of Adilabad, the Andhra Pradesh state police fired a bullet into the chest of a man called Cherukuri Rajkumar, known to his comrades as Azad. Azad was a member of the Politburo of the banned Communist Party of India (Maoist), and had been nominated by his party as its chief negotiator for the proposed peace talks with the Government of India.

Why did the police fire at point-blank range and leave those telltale burn marks when they could so easily have covered their tracks? Was it a mistake or was it a message?

They killed a second person that morning—Hemchandra Pandey, a young journalist who was travelling with Azad when he was apprehended. Why did they kill him? Was it to make sure no eyewitness remained alive to tell the tale? Or was it just whimsy?

In the course of a war, if, in the preliminary stages of a peace negotiation, one side executes the envoy of the other side, it's reasonable to assume that the side that did the killing does not want peace. It looks very much as though Azad was killed because someone decided that the stakes were too high to allow him to remain alive. That decision could turn out to be a serious error of judgement. Not just because of who he was, but because of the political climate in India today.

Trickledown Revolution

Days after I said goodbye to the comrades
and emerged from Dandakaranya forest, I
found myself charting a weary but familiar
course to Jantar Mantar, on Parliament
Street in New Delhi. Jantar Mantar is an
old observatory built by Maharaja Sawai Jai
Singh II of Jaipur in the eighteenth century.
In those days it was a scientific marvel, used
to tell the time, predict the weather and
study the planets. Today it's a not-so-hot
tourist attraction that doubles up as Delhi's
little showroom for democracy.

For some years now, protests—unless they're patronized by political parties or religious organizations—have been banned in Delhi. The Boat Club on Rajpath, which has in the past seen huge, historic rallies that sometimes lasted for days, is out of bounds for political activity now, and is only available for picnics, balloon-sellers and boat rides. As for India Gate, candlelight vigils and boutique protests for middle-class causes—such as 'Justice for Jessica', the model who was killed in a Delhi bar by a thug with political connections—are allowed, but nothing more. Section 144, an old nineteenth-century law that bans the gathering of more than five people—who have 'a common object which is unlawful'—in a public place has been clamped on the city. The law was passed by the British in 1860 to prevent a repeat of the 1857 Mutiny. It was meant to be an emergency measure, but has become a permanent fixture in many parts of India. Perhaps it was in gratitude for laws like these that our prime minister, while accepting an honorary degree from Oxford, thanked the British for bequeathing us such a rich legacy: 'Our judiciary, our legal system, our bureaucracy and our police are all great institutions, derived from British-Indian administration and they have served the country well.'[2]

Jantar Mantar is the only place in Delhi where Section 144 applies but is not enforced. People from all over the country, fed up with being ignored by the political establishment and the media, converge there, desperately hoping for a hearing. Some take long train journeys. Some, like the victims of the Bhopal gas leak, have walked for weeks all the way to Delhi. Though they had to fight each other for the best spot on the burning (or freezing) pavement, until recently protestors were allowed to camp in Jantar Mantar for as long as they liked—weeks, months, even years. Under the malevolent gaze of the police and the Special Branch, they would put up their faded shamianas and banners. From here they declared their faith in democracy by issuing their memoranda, announcing their protest plans and staging their indefinite hunger strikes. From here they tried (but never succeeded) to march on Parliament. From here they hoped.

Of late, though, Democracy's timings have been changed. It's strictly office hours now, nine to five. No overtime. No sleepovers. No matter from how far people have come, no matter if they have no shelter in the city, if they don't leave by 6 p.m. they are forcibly dispersed, by the police if necessary, with batons and water canons if things get out of hand. The new timings were ostensibly instituted to make sure that the 2010 Commonwealth Games in New Delhi would go smoothly. But nobody's expecting the old timings back any time soon. Maybe it's in the fitness of things that what's left of our democracy should be traded in for an event that was created to celebrate the British Empire. Perhaps it's only right that nearly 400,000 people should have been driven out of the city and many seen their homes demolished.[3] Or that hundreds of thousands of roadside vendors should have had their livelihoods snatched away by order of the Supreme Court so city malls could take over their share of business.[4] And that tens of thousands of beggars should have been shipped out of the city while more than a hundred thousand galley slaves were shipped in to build the flyovers, metro tunnels, Olympic-size swimming pools, warm-up stadiums and luxury housing for athletes.[5] The Old Empire may not exist. But obviously our tradition of servility has become too profitable an enterprise to dismantle.

I was at Jantar Mantar in spring 2010 because a thousand pavement dwellers from cities all over the country had come to demand a few fundamental rights: the right to shelter, to food (ration cards), to life (protection from police brutality and criminal extortion by municipal officers).

The sun was sharp that day, but still civilized. This is a terrible thing to have to say, but it's true—you could smell the protest from a fair distance: it was the accumulated odour of a thousand human bodies that had been dehumanized, denied the basic necessities for human (or even animal) health and hygiene for years, if not a whole lifetime. Bodies that had been marinated in the refuse of our big cities, bodies that had no shelter from the harsh weather, no access to clean water, clean air, sanitation or medical care. No part of this great country, none of the supposedly progressive schemes, no single urban institution has been designed to accommodate them. Not the Jawaharlal Nehru National Urban Renewal Mission, not any other slum development, employment guarantee or welfare scheme. Not even the sewage system—they shit on *top* of it. They are shadow people, who live in the cracks that run between schemes and institutions. They sleep on the streets, eat on the streets, make love on the streets, give birth on the streets, are raped on the streets, cut their vegetables, wash their clothes, raise their children, live and die on the streets.

153

If the motion picture were an art form that involved the olfactory senses—in other words, if cinema smelled—then films like *Slumdog Millionaire* would not win Oscars. The stench of that kind of poverty wouldn't blend with the aroma of warm popcorn.

The people at the protest in Jantar Mantar that day were not even slum dogs, they were pavement dwellers. Who were they? Where had they come from? They were the refugees of India Shining, the people who are being sloshed around like toxic effluent in a manufacturing process that has gone berserk. The representatives of the estimated sixty million people who have been displaced by rural destitution, by slow starvation, by floods and drought (many of them man-made), by mines, steel factories and aluminium smelters, by highways and expressways, by the 3300 big dams built since Independence, and now by special economic zones (SEZs). They're part of the 836 million people of India who live on less than twenty rupees a day, the ones who starve while millions of tonnes of food grain is either eaten by rats in government warehouses or burnt in bulk (because it's cheaper to burn food than to distribute it to poor people).[6] They're the parents of the tens of millions of malnourished children in our country, of the 1.5 million who die every year before they reach their first birthday.[7] They're the millions who make up the chain gangs that are transported from city to city to build the New India. Is this what is known as 'enjoying the fruits of modern development'?

What must they think, these people, about a government that sees fit to spend 240 billion rupees of public money (the initial estimate was 4 billion rupees) for a two-week-long sports extravaganza which, for fear of terrorism, malaria, dengue and New Delhi's new superbug, many international athletes have refused to attend?[8] Which the Queen of England, titular head of the Commonwealth, would not consider presiding over, not even in her most irresponsible dreams. What must they think of the fact that enormous sums of money has been stolen and salted away by politicians and Games officials? Not much, I guess. Because for people who live on less than twenty rupees a day, money on that scale must seem like science fiction. Maybe it doesn't occur to them that it's *their* money. That's why corrupt politicians in India never have a problem sweeping back into power, using the money they stole to buy elections. (Then they feign outrage and ask, 'Why don't the Maoists stand for elections?')

Standing at Jantar Mantar on that bright day, I thought of all the struggles that are being waged by people in this country—against big dams in the Narmada Valley, Polavaram, Arunachal Pradesh; against mines in Orissa, Chhattisgarh, Jharkhand; against the police by the adivasis of Lalgarh; against the grabbing of their lands for industries and special economic zones all over the country. How many years and in how many ways have people fought to avoid just such a fate? I thought of Maase, Narmada, Roopi, Niti, Mangtu, Madhav, Saroja, Raju, Gudsa Usendi and Comrade Kamla with their guns slung over their shoulders. I thought of the great dignity of the forest I had so recently walked in and the rhythm of the adivasi drums at the Bhumkal celebration in Bastar, like the soundtrack of the quickening pulse of a furious nation.

HIGHWAY TO PARADIP, KEONJHAR, ORISSA 2005

Red dust fills your nostrils and lungs. The water is red, the air is red, the people are red, their lungs and hair are red. All day and all night trucks rumble through their villages, bumper to bumper, thousands and thousands of trucks, taking ore to Paradip port from where it will go to China. There it will turn into cars and smoke and sudden cities that spring up overnight.

PROTEST AGAINST BODHGHAT DAM,
DANDAKARANYA, 2010
More than 60 million people
have been displaced by rural
destitution, by slow starvation,
by floods and drought, by mines,
steel factories and aluminium
smelters, by highways and
expressways, by the 3300 big
dams built since Independence
and now by special
economic zones.

I thought of Padma with whom I travelled to Warangal. She's only in her thirties, but she has to hold the banister and drag her body behind her when she walks up stairs. She was arrested just a week after she had had an appendix operation. She was beaten until she had an internal haemorrhage and severe organ damage. When they cracked her knees, the police explained helpfully that it was to make sure 'she would never walk in the jungle again'. She was released after serving an eight-year sentence. Now she runs the Amarula Bandhu Mithrula Sangham, the Committee of Relatives and Friends of Martyrs. It retrieves the bodies of people killed in fake encounters. Padma spends her time crisscrossing northern Andhra Pradesh in whatever transport she can find, usually a tractor, transporting the corpses of people whose parents or spouses are too poor to make the journey to retrieve the bodies of their loved ones.

The tenacity, the wisdom and the courage of those who have been fighting for years, for decades, to bring change, or even the whisper of justice to their lives, is something extraordinary. Whether people are fighting to overthrow the Indian State or fighting against Big Dams or only fighting a particular steel plant or mine or SEZ, the bottom line is that they are fighting for their dignity, for the right to live and smell like human beings. They're fighting because, as far as they're concerned, 'the fruits of modern development' stink like dead cattle on the highway.

~

On the sixty-third anniversary of India's Independence, Prime Minister Manmohan Singh climbed into his bullet-proof soap box in the Red Fort to deliver a passionless, bone-chillingly banal speech to the nation. Listening to him, who would have guessed that he was addressing a country that, despite having the second highest economic growth rate in the world, has more poor people in just eight of its states than in the twenty-six countries of sub-Saharan Africa put together?[9] 'All of you have contributed to India's success,' he said.

> The hard work of our workers, our artisans, our farmers has brought our country to where it stands today ... We are building a new India in which every citizen would have a stake, an India which would be prosperous and in which all citizens would be able to live a life of honour and dignity in an environment of peace and goodwill. An India in which all problems could be solved through democratic means. An India in which the basic rights of every citizen would be protected.[10]

Some would call this graveyard humour. He might as well have been speaking to people in Finland or Sweden.

If our prime minister's reputation for 'personal integrity' extended to the text of his speeches, this is what he should have said:

Brothers and sisters, greetings to you on this day on which we remember our glorious past. Things are getting a little expensive, I know, and you keep complaining about food prices. But look at it this way—more than 650 million of you are engaged in and are living off agriculture as farmers and farm labour, but your combined efforts contribute less than 18 per cent of our GDP. So what's the use of you? Look at our IT sector. It employs 0.2 per cent of the population and earns us 5 per cent of our national income.[11] Can you match that? It is true that employment hasn't kept pace with growth in our country, but fortunately more than 60 per cent of our workforce is self-employed.[12] Ninety per cent of our labour force is employed by the unorganized sector.[13] True, they manage to get work only for a few months in the year, but since we don't have a category called 'underemployed' we just keep that part a little vague. It would not be right to enter them in our books as unemployed. Coming to the statistics that say we have among the highest infant and maternal mortality rates in the world, we should unite as a nation and ignore bad news for the time being. We can address these problems later, after our Trickledown Revolution, when the health sector has been completely privatized. Meanwhile, I hope you are all buying medical insurance. As for the fact that the per capita food grain availability actually decreased during the period of some of our most rapid economic growth—believe me, that's just a coincidence.[14]

My fellow citizens, we are building a new India in which our 100 richest people hold assets worth one fourth of our GDP.[15] Wealth concentrated in fewer and fewer hands is always more efficient. You have all heard the saying that too many cooks spoil the broth. We want our beloved billionaires, our few hundred millionaires, their near and dear ones and their political and business associates, to be prosperous and to live a life of honour and dignity in an environment of peace and goodwill in which their basic rights are protected.[16]

I am aware that my dreams cannot come true by solely using democratic means. In fact, I have come to believe that real democracy flows through the barrel of a gun. This is why we have deployed the army, the police, the Central Reserve Police Force, the Border Security Force, the Central Industrial Security Force, the Pradeshik Armed Constabulary, the Indo-Tibetan Border Police, the Eastern Frontier Rifles—as well as the Scorpions, Greyhounds and Cobras—to crush the misguided insurrections that are erupting in our mineral-rich areas.

Our experiments with democracy began in Nagaland, Manipur and Kashmir. Kashmir, I need not reiterate, is an integral part of India. We have deployed more than half a million soldiers to bring democracy to the people there. The Kashmiri youth who have been risking their lives by defying curfew and throwing stones at the police for the last two months are Lashkar-e-Taiba militants who actually want employment, not azadi. Tragically, sixty of them lost their lives before we could study their job applications. I have instructed the police from now on to shoot to maim rather than kill these misguided youths.

In his seven years in office, Manmohan Singh has allowed himself to be cast as Sonia Gandhi's tentative, mild-mannered underling. It's an excellent disguise for a man who, for the last twenty years, first as finance minister and then as prime minister, has powered through a regime of new economic policies that has brought India into the situation in which it finds itself now. This is not to suggest that Manmohan Singh is not an underling. Only that all his orders don't come from Sonia Gandhi. In his autobiography, *A Prattler's Tale*, Ashok Mitra, former finance minister of West Bengal, tells his story of how Manmohan Singh rose to power.[17] In 1991, when India's foreign exchange reserves were dangerously low, the P.V. Narasimha Rao government approached the International Monetary Fund (IMF) for an emergency loan. The IMF agreed on two conditions. The first was structural adjustment and economic reform. The second was the appointment of a finance minister of its choice. That man, says Mitra, was Manmohan Singh.

Over the years, Singh has stacked his cabinet and the bureaucracy with people who are evangelically committed to the corporate takeover of everything—water, electricity, minerals, agriculture, land, telecommunications, education, health—no matter what the consequences.

Sonia Gandhi and her son play an important part in all of this. Their job is to run the Department of Compassion and Charisma—and to win elections. They are allowed to make (and also to take credit for) decisions which appear progressive but are actually tactical and symbolic, meant to take the edge off popular anger and allow the big ship to keep on rolling. (The most recent example of this is the rally that was organized for Rahul Gandhi to claim victory for the cancellation of Vedanta's permission to mine Niyamgiri for bauxite—a battle that the Dongria Kondh tribe and a coalition of activists, local as well as international, have been fighting for years. At the rally, Rahul Gandhi announced that he was a 'soldier' for the tribal people.[18] He didn't mention that the economic policies of his party are predicated on the mass displacement of tribal people. Or that every other bauxite *giri*—hill—in the neighbourhood was having the hell mined out of it, while this 'soldier' for the tribal people looked away. Rahul Gandhi may be a decent man. But for him to go around talking about the 'Two Indias'—the 'Rich India' and the 'Poor India'—as though the party he represents has nothing to do with this fact, is an insult to everybody's intelligence, including his own.)

The division of labour between politicians who have a mass base, and win elections to keep the charade of democracy going, and those who actually run the country but either do not need to (judges and bureaucrats) or have been freed of the constraint of winning elections (like the prime minister) is a brilliant subversion of democratic practice. To imagine that Sonia and Rahul Gandhi are in charge of the government would be a mistake. The real power has passed into the hands of a coven of oligarchs—judges, bureaucrats, politicians. They in turn are run like prize racehorses by the few corporations who more or less own everything in the country. They may belong to different political parties and put up a great show of being political rivals, but that's just subterfuge for public consumption. The only real rivalry is the business rivalry between corporations.

A senior member of the coven is P. Chidambaram, who some say is so popular with the Opposition that he may continue to be home minister even if the Congress were to lose the next election. That's probably just as well. He may need a few extra years in office to complete the task he has been assigned. But it doesn't matter if he stays or goes. The die has been rolled.

In a lecture at Harvard, his old university, in October 2007, Chidambaram outlined that task. The lecture was called 'Poor Rich Countries: The Challenges of Development'.[19] He called the first three decades after Independence the 'lost decades' and exulted about the GDP growth rate which has grown an average of 6.9 per cent annually in the years 2000 to 2007. What he said is important enough for me to inflict a chunk of his charmless prose on you:

TOXIC EFFLUENTS IN THE EARTH, DAMANJODI, ORISSA

The financial value of the bauxite deposits of Orissa alone is
4 trillion dollars (much more than twice India's gross domestic
product) ... Of this, officially the government gets a royalty of
less than 7 per cent.

TOXIC AIR, DAMANJODI, ORISSA
There is no environmentally
sustainable way of mining
bauxite and processing it into
aluminium. It's a highly toxic
process that most Western
countries have exported out of
their own environments.

One would have thought that the challenge of development—in a democracy—will become less formidable as the economy cruises on a high growth path. The reality is the opposite. Democracy—rather, the institutions of democracy—and the legacy of the socialist era have actually added to the challenge of development.

Let me explain with some examples. India's mineral resources include coal—the fourth largest reserves in the world—iron ore, manganese, mica, bauxite, titanium ore, chromite, diamonds, natural gas, petroleum, and limestone. Commonsense tells us that we should mine these resources quickly and efficiently. That requires huge capital, efficient organizations and a policy environment that will allow market forces to operate. None of these factors is present today in the mining sector. The laws in this behalf are outdated and Parliament has been able to only tinker at the margins. Our efforts to attract private investment in prospecting and mining have, by and large, failed. Meanwhile, the sector remains virtually captive in the hands of the State governments. Opposing any change in the status quo are groups that espouse—quite legitimately—the cause of the forests or the environment or the tribal population. There are also political parties that regard mining as a natural monopoly of the State and have ideological objections to the entry of the private sector. They garner support from the established trade unions. Behind the unions—either known or unknown to them—stand the trading mafia. The result: actual investment is low, the mining sector grows at a tardy pace and it acts as a drag on the economy.

I shall give you another example. Vast extent of land is required for locating industries. Mineral-based industries such as steel and aluminium require large tracts of land for mining, processing and production. Infrastructure projects like airports, seaports, dams and power stations need very large extents of land so that they can provide road and rail connectivity and the ancillary and support facilities. Hitherto, land was acquired by the governments in exercise of the power of eminent domain. The only issue was payment of adequate compensation. That situation has changed. There are new stakeholders in every project, and their claims have to be recognized. We are now obliged to address issues such as environmental impact assessment, justification for compulsory acquisition, right compensation, solatium, rehabilitation and resettlement of the displaced persons, alternative house sites and farm land, and one job for each affected family.

Allowing 'market forces' to mine resources 'quickly and efficiently' is what colonizers did to their colonies, what Spain and North America did to South America, what Europe did (and continues to do) in Africa. It's what the Apartheid regime did in South Africa. What puppet dictators in small countries do to bleed their people. It's a formula for growth and development, but for *someone else*. It's an old, old, old, old story—must we really go over that ground again?

Now that mining licences have been issued with the urgency you'd associate with a knock-down distress sale, and the scams that are emerging have run into billions of dollars, now that mining companies have polluted rivers, mined away state borders, wrecked ecosystems and unleashed civil war, the consequence of what the coven has set into motion is playing out like an ancient lament over ruined landscapes and the bodies of the poor.

Note the regret with which the minister in his lecture talks about democracy and the obligations it entails: 'Democracy—rather, the institutions of democracy—and the legacy of the socialist era have actually added to the challenge of development.' He follows that up with a standard-issue clutch of subterfuge about compensation, rehabilitation and jobs. *What* compensation? *What* solatium? *What* rehabilitation? And *what* 'job for each affected family'? As for being 'obliged' to provide 'justification' for the 'compulsory acquisition' of land, a cabinet minister surely knows that to compulsorily acquire tribal land (which is where most of the minerals are) and turn it over to private mining corporations is illegal and unconstitutional under the Panchayat (Extension to Scheduled Areas) Act. Passed in 1996, PESA is an amendment that attempts to right some of the wrongs done to tribal people by the Indian Constitution when it was adopted by Parliament in 1950. It overrides all existing laws that may be in conflict with it. It is a law that acknowledges the deepening marginalization of tribal communities and is meant to radically recast the balance of power. As a piece of legislation, it is unique because it makes the community—the collective—a legal entity and it confers on tribal societies that live in scheduled areas the right to self-governance. Under PESA, 'compulsory acquisition' of tribal land cannot be justified on any count. So, ironically, those who are being called 'Maoists' (which includes everyone who is resisting land acquisition) are actually fighting to uphold the Constitution while the government is doing its best to vandalize it.

171

Between 2008 and 2009 the Ministry of Panchayati Raj commissioned two researchers to write a chapter for a report on the progress of Panchayati Raj in the country. The chapter is called 'PESA, Left Wing Extremism and Governance: Concerns and Challenges in India's Tribal Districts', its authors are Ajay Dandekar and Chitrangada Choudhury.[20] Here are some extracts:

> The central Land Acquisition Act of 1894 has till date not been amended to bring it in line with the provisions of PESA ... At the moment, this colonial-era law is being widely misused on the ground to forcibly acquire individual and community land for private industry. In several cases, the practice of the state government is to sign high profile MOUs with corporate houses and then proceed to deploy the Acquisition Act to ostensibly acquire the land for the state industrial corporation. This body then simply leases the land to the private corporation—a complete travesty of the term 'acquisition for a public purpose', as sanctioned by the act....
>
> There are cases where the formal resolutions of gram sabha expressing dissent have been destroyed and substituted by forged documents. What is worse, no action has been taken by the

state against concerned officials even after the facts got established. The message is clear and ominous. There is collusion in these deals at numerous levels....

The sale of tribal lands to non-tribals in the Schedule V areas is prohibited in all these states. However, transfers continue to take place and have become more perceptible in the post liberalization era. The principal reasons are—transfer through fraudulent means, unrecorded transfers on the basis of oral transactions, transfers by misrepresentation of facts and mis-stating the purpose, forcible occupation of tribal lands, transfer through illegal marriages, collusive title suites, incorrect recording at the time of the survey, land acquisition process, eviction of encroachments and in the name of exploitation of timber and forest produce and even on the pretext of development of welfarism.

The authors conclude:

The Memorandum of Understandings signed by the state governments with industrial houses, including mining companies should be re-examined in a public exercise, with gram sabhas at the centre of this enquiry.

Here it is then—not troublesome activists, not the Maoists, but a government report calling for the mining MoUs to be re-examined. What does the government do with this document? How does it respond? On 24 April 2010, at a formal ceremony, the prime minister released the report. Brave of him, you'd think. Except, this chapter wasn't in it. It was dropped.[21]

Half a century ago, just a year before he was killed, Che Guevara wrote: 'When the oppressive forces come to maintain themselves in power against established law, peace is considered already broken.'[22] Indeed it must. In 2009 Manmohan Singh said in Parliament, 'If Left Wing extremism continues to flourish in important parts of our country which have tremendous natural resources of minerals and other precious things, that will certainly affect the climate for investment.'[23] This was a furtive declaration of war.

(Permit me a small digression here, a moment to tell a very short Tale of Two Sikhs: In his last petition to the Punjab Governor, before he was hanged by the British government in 1931, Bhagat Singh, the celebrated revolutionary—and Marxist—said, 'Let us declare that the state of war does exist and shall exist so long as the Indian toiling masses and the natural resources are being exploited by a handful of parasites. They may be purely British Capitalist or mixed British and Indian or even purely Indian…. All these things make no difference.'[24])

If you pay attention to many of the struggles taking place in India, people are demanding no more than their constitutional rights. But the Government of India no longer feels it needs to abide by the Indian Constitution, which is supposed to be the legal and moral framework on which our democracy rests. As constitutions go, it is an enlightened document, but its enlightenment is not used to protect people. Quite the opposite. It is used as a spiked club to beat down those who are protesting against the growing tide of violence being perpetrated by a state on its people in the name of the 'public good'. In a recent article in *Outlook*, B.G. Verghese, a senior journalist, came out waving that club in defence of the state and big corporations: 'The Maoists will fade away, democratic India and the Constitution will prevail, despite the time it takes and the pain involved.'[25] To this, Azad replied (it was the last piece he wrote before he was murdered):

> In which part of India is the Constitution prevailing, Mr. Verghese? In Dantewada, Bijapur, Kanker, Narayanpur, Rajnandgaon? In Jharkhand, Orissa? In Lalgarh, Jangalmahal? In the Kashmir Valley? Manipur? Where was your Constitution hiding for 25 long years after thousand of Sikhs were massacred? When

thousands of Muslims were decimated? When lakhs of peasants are compelled to commit suicides? When thousands of people are murdered by state-sponsored Salwa Judum gangs? When adivasi women are gangraped? When people are simply abducted by uniformed goons? Your Constitution is a piece of paper that does not even have the value of a toilet paper for the vast majority of the Indian people.[26]

After Azad was killed, several media commentators tried to paper over the crime by shamelessly inverting what he had said, accusing him of calling the Indian Constitution a piece of toilet paper.

If the government won't respect the Constitution, perhaps we should push for an amendment to the preamble. 'We, the People of India, having solemnly resolved to constitute India into a Sovereign Socialist Secular Democratic Republic...' could be substituted with 'We, the upper castes and classes of India, having secretly resolved to constitute India into a Corporate, Hindu, Satellite State...'

~

The insurrection in the Indian countryside, in particular in the tribal heartland, poses a radical challenge not only to the Indian State, but to resistance movements too. It questions the accepted ideas of what constitutes progress, development and indeed civilization itself. It questions the ethics, as well as the effectiveness, of different strategies of resistance. These questions have been asked before, yes. They have been asked persistently, peacefully, year after year in a hundred different ways—by the Chhattisgarh Mukti Morcha, the Koel Karo and Gandhamardhan agitations—and hundreds of other people's movements. It was asked most persuasively, and perhaps most visibly, by the Narmada Bachao Andolan, the anti-dam movement in the Narmada Valley. The Government of India's only answer has been repression, deviousness and the kind of opacity that can only come from a pathological disrespect for ordinary people. Worse, it went ahead and accelerated the process of displacement and dispossession to a point when people's anger has built up in ways that cannot be controlled. Today the poorest people in the world have managed to stop some of the richest corporations in their tracks. It's a huge victory.

Those who have risen up are aware that their country is in a state of emergency. They are aware that like the people of Kashmir, Manipur, Nagaland and Assam they too have now been stripped of their civil rights by laws like the Unlawful Activities (Prevention)

MILITIA AT BHUMKAL, DANDAKARANYA, 2010

How in god's name will the security forces be able to distinguish a Maoist from an ordinary person who is running terrified through the jungle? Will adivasis carrying the bows and arrows they have carried for centuries now count as Maoists too?

A PHOTO EXHIBITION OF MARTYRS
OF THE MOVEMENT, BHUMKAL,
DANDAKARANYA 2010

Chairman Mao. He's here too.
A little lonely, perhaps, but present.
There's a photograph of him, up on
a red cloth screen. Marx too. And
Charu Mazumdar, the founder and
chief theoretician of the Naxalite
movement. His abrasive rhetoric
fetishizes violence, blood and
martyrdom, and often employs a
language so coarse as to be almost
genocidal. Standing here, on
Bhumkal day, I can't help thinking
that his analysis, so vital to the
structure of this revolution,
is so removed from its emotion
and texture.

Act and the Chhattisgarh Special Public Security Act, which criminalize every kind of dissent—by word, deed and even *intent*.

When Indira Gandhi declared the Emergency at midnight on 25 June 1975, she did it to crush an incipient revolution. As grim as they were, those were days when people still allowed themselves to dream of bettering their lot, to dream of justice. The Naxalite uprising in Bengal had been more or less decimated. But then millions of people rallied to Jayaprakash Narayan's call for 'Sampoorna Kranti' (Total Revolution). At the heart of all the unrest was the demand for land to the tiller. (Even back then it was no different—you needed a revolution to implement land redistribution, which is one of the directive principles of the Constitution.)

Thirty-five years later, things have changed drastically. Justice, that grand, beautiful idea, has been whittled down to mean human rights. Equality is a utopian fantasy. That word has been more or less evicted from our vocabulary. The poor have been pushed to the wall. From fighting for land for the landless, revolutionary parties and resistance movements have had to lower their sights to fighting for people's rights to hold on to what little land they have. The only kind of land redistribution that seems to be on the cards is the land being grabbed from the poor and redistributed to the rich for their land banks, which go under the name of special economic zones. The landless (mostly Dalits), the jobless, the slum dwellers and the urban working class are more or less out of the reckoning. In places like Lalgarh in West Bengal, people are only asking the police and the government to leave them alone. The adivasi organization called the People's Committee against Police Atrocities (PCAPA) began with one simple demand—that the superintendent of police visit Lalgarh and apologize to the people for the atrocities his men had committed on villagers. That was considered preposterous. (How could half-naked savages expect a government *officer* to apologize to them?) So people barricaded their villages and refused to let the police in. The police stepped up the violence. People responded with fury. Now, two years down the line, and many gruesome rapes, killings and fake encounters later, it's all-out war. The PCAPA has been banned and dubbed a Maoist outfit. Its leaders have been jailed or shot. (A similar fate has befallen the Chasi Mulia Adivasi Sangh in Narayanpatna in Orissa and the Visthapen Virodhi Ekta Manch in Potka in Jharkhand.)

People who once dreamed of justice and equality, and dared to demand land to the tiller, have been reduced to asking for an apology from the police for being beaten and maimed. Is this progress?

During the Emergency, the saying goes, when Mrs

Gandhi asked the press to bend, it crawled. And yet, in those days, there were instances when national dailies defiantly published blank editorials to protest censorship. (Irony of ironies—one of those defiant editors was B.G. Verghese.) This time around, in the undeclared emergency, there's not much scope for defiance because the media *is* the government. Nobody, except the corporations who control it, can tell it what to do. Senior politicians, ministers and officers of the security establishment vie to appear on TV, feebly imploring news anchors for permission to interrupt the day's sermon. Several TV channels and newspapers are overtly manning Operation Green Hunt's war room and its disinformation campaign. There was the identically worded story about the '1,500 crore Maoist industry' filed under the byline of different reporters in several different papers.[27] Almost all newspapers and TV channels ran stories blaming the PCAPA (used interchangeably with 'Maoists') for the horrific train derailment in Jhargram in West Bengal in May 2010 in which 150 people died. Two of the main suspects have been shot down by the police in 'encounters', even though the mystery around the train accident is still unravelling. The Press Trust of India put out several untruthful stories, faithfully showcased by the *Indian Express*, including one about Maoists mutilating the bodies of policemen they had killed.[28] (The denial, which came from the police themselves, was published postage-stamp size, hidden in the middle pages.) There are the several identical interviews, all of them billed as 'exclusive', with the female guerrilla about how she had been raped repeatedly by Maoist leaders.[29] She was supposed to have recently escaped from the forests and the clutches of the Maoists to tell the world her tale. Now it turns out that she has been in police custody for months.

The atrocity-based analyses shouted out at us from our TV screens are designed to smoke up the mirrors, and hustle us into thinking, 'Yes, the tribals have been neglected and are having a very bad time. Yes, they need development. Yes, it's the government's fault, and it's a great pity. But right now there is a crisis. We need to get rid of the Maoists, secure the land and then we can help the tribals.'

As war closes in, the armed forces have announced, in the way only they can, that they too are getting into the business of messing with our heads. In June 2010 they released two 'operational doctrines'.[30] One was a joint doctrine for air–land operations. The other was a doctrine on Military Psychological Operations, which 'constitutes a planned process of conveying a message to select target audience, to promote particular themes that result in desired attitudes and behaviour, which affect the achievement of political and military objectives of the country'. In addition, 'The Doctrine also provides guidelines for activities related to perception management in sub conventional operations, specially in an internal environment wherein misguided population may have to be brought into the mainstream.' According to the Press Trust of India, 'The doctrine on Military Psychological Operations is a policy, planning and implementation document that aims to create a conducive environment for the armed forces to operate by using the media available with the Services to their advantage'.

A month later, at a meeting of chief ministers of Naxalite-affected states, a decision was taken to escalate the war. Thirty-six battalions of the India Reserve Force were added to the existing 105 battalions, and 16,000 special police officers (civilians armed and contracted to function as police) were added to the existing 30,000. The Home Secretary promised to hire 800,000 policemen over the next five years.[31] (It's a good model for an employment guarantee scheme: hire half the population to shoot the other half. You can fool around with the ratios if you like.)

A few days later, the Army Chief told his senior officers to 'be mentally prepared to step into the fight against Naxalism.... It might be in six months or in a year or two, but if we have to maintain our relevance as a tool of the state, we will have to undertake things that the nation wants us to do.'[32]

By August, newspapers were reporting that the on-again-off-again air force was on again. 'The IAF [Indian Air Force] can fire in self-defence during anti-Maoist operations' the *Hindustan Times* reported.[33] An unnamed source told the Indo-Asian News Service, 'The permission has been granted but with strict conditionalities. We cannot use rockets or the integral guns of the helicopters and we can retaliate only if fired upon … To this end, we have side-mounted machineguns on our choppers that are operated by our Garuds (IAF commandoes).' That's a relief. No integral guns, only side-mounted machineguns.

Maybe 'six months or in a year or two' is about as long as it will take for the brigade headquarters in Bilaspur and the air base in Rajnandgaon to be ready. Maybe by then, in a great show of democratic spirit, the government will give in to popular anger and repeal AFSPA, the Armed Forces (Special Powers) Act (which allows non-commissioned officers to kill on suspicion), in Manipur, Nagaland, Assam and Kashmir. Once the applause subsides and the celebration peters out, AFSPA will be recast, as the home minister has suggested, on the lines of the Jeevan Reddy report (to sound more humane but to be more deadly).[34] Then it can be promulgated all over the country under a new name. Maybe that will give the armed forces the impunity they need to do what 'the nation' wants them to do—to be deployed in parts of India against the poorest of the poor who are fighting for their very survival.[35]

Maybe that's how Comrade Kamla will die—while she's trying to bring down a helicopter gunship or a military training jet with her pistol. Or maybe by then she will have graduated to an AK-47 or a light machine gun looted from a government armory or a murdered policeman. Maybe by then the media 'available to the Services' will have 'managed' the perceptions of those of us who still continue to be 'misguided' to receive the news of her death with equanimity.

So here's the Indian State, in all its democratic glory, willing to loot, starve, lay siege to, and now deploy the air force in 'self-defence' against its poorest citizens.

Self-defence. Ah, yes. Operation Green Hunt is being waged in self-defence by a government that is trying to restore land to poor people whose land has been snatched away by Commie Corporations.

When the government uses the offer of peace talks to draw the deep-swimming fish up to the surface and then kill them, do peace talks have a future? Is either side genuinely interested in peace? Are the Maoists really interested in peace or justice, people ask; is there anything they can be offered within the existing system that will deflect the Maoists from their stated goal of overthrowing the Indian State? The answer to that is probably not. The Maoists do not believe that the present system can deliver justice. The thing is that an increasing number of people are beginning to agree with them. If we lived in a society with a genuinely democratic impulse, one in which ordinary people felt they could at least *hope* for justice, then the Maoists would only be a small, marginalized group of militants with very little popular appeal.

The other contention is that Maoists want a ceasefire to take the heat off themselves for a while so that they can use the time to regroup and consolidate their position. In an interview, Azad was surprisingly candid about this: 'It doesn't need much of a common sense to understand that both sides will utilize a situation of ceasefire to strengthen their respective sides.'[36] He then went on to explain that a ceasefire, even a temporary one, would give respite to ordinary people who are caught in a war zone.

The government, on the other hand, desperately needs this war. (Read the business papers to see *how* desperately.) The eyes of the international business community are boring holes into its back. It needs to deliver, and fast. To keep its mask from falling, it must continue to offer talks on the one hand, and undermine them on the other. The elimination of Azad was an important victory because it silenced a voice that had begun to sound dangerously reasonable. For the moment at least, peace talks have been successfully derailed.

There is plenty to be cynical about in the discussion around peace talks. The thing for us ordinary folks to remember is that no peace talks means an escalating war.

~

Over the last few months, the government has poured tens of thousands of heavily armed paramilitary troops into the forest. The Maoists responded with a series of aggressive attacks and ambushes. More than 200 policemen have been killed.[37] The bodies keep coming out of the forest. Slain policemen wrapped in the national flag; slain Maoists, displayed like hunter's trophies, their wrists and ankles lashed to bamboo poles; bullet-ridden bodies, bodies that don't look human any more, mutilated in ambushes, beheadings and summary executions. (Of the bodies being buried *in* the forest, we have no news.) The theatre of war has been cordoned off, closed to activists and journalists. So there are no body counts.

On 6 April 2010, in its biggest strike ever, in Dantewada the Maoists' People's Liberation Guerrilla Army (PLGA) ambushed a Central Reserve Police Force

(CRPF) company and killed seventy-six policemen.[38] The party issued a coldly triumphant statement.[39] Television milked the tragedy for everything it was worth. The nation was called upon to condemn the killing. Many of us were not prepared to—not because we celebrate killing, nor because we are all Maoists, but because we have thorny, knotty views about Operation Green Hunt. For refusing to buy shares in the rapidly growing condemnation industry, we were branded 'terrorist sympathizers' and had our photographs flashed repeatedly on TV like wanted criminals.

AT AN AGRICULTURAL FAIR, A STYROFOAM MODEL PROMOTES MINING UTOPIA. We're watching a democracy trying to eat its own limbs. And those limbs are refusing to be eaten.

What was a CRPF contingent doing, patrolling tribal villages with twenty-one AK-47 rifles, thirty-eight INSAS rifles, seven self-loading rifles, six light machine guns, one Sten gun and one 2-inch mortar?[40] To ask that question almost amounted to an act of treason.

Days after the ambush, I ran into two paramilitary commandos chatting to a bunch of drivers in a Delhi car park. They were waiting for their VIP to emerge from some restaurant or health club or hotel. Their view on what is going on involved neither grief nor patriotism. It was simple accounting. A balance sheet. They were talking about how many hundreds of thousands of rupees in bribes it takes for a man to get a job in the paramilitary forces, and how most families incur huge debts to pay that bribe. That debt can never be repaid by the pathetic wages paid to a jawan, for example. The only way to repay it is to do what policemen in India do—blackmail and threaten people, run protection rackets, demand pay-offs, do dirty deals. (In the case of Dantewada, loot villagers, steal cash and jewellery.) But if the man dies an untimely death, it leaves the families hugely in debt. The anger of the men in the car park was directed at the government and senior police officers who make fortunes from bribes and then so casually send young men to their death. They knew that the handsome compensation that was announced for the dead in the 6 April attack was just to blunt the impact of the scandal. It was never going to be standard practice for every policeman who dies in this sordid war.

Small wonder then that the news from the war zone is that CRPF men are increasingly reluctant to go on patrol. There are reports of them fudging their daily logbooks, filling them with phantom patrols.[41] Maybe they're beginning to realize that they are only poor khaki trash—cannon fodder in a rich man's war. There are thousands waiting to replace each one of them when they're gone.

On 17 May 2010, in another major attack, the Maoists blew up a bus in Dantewada and killed about forty-four people.[42] Of them eighteen were special police officers (SPOs), members of the dreaded government-sponsored people's militia, the Salwa Judum. The rest of the dead were, shockingly, ordinary people, mostly adivasis. The Maoists expressed perfunctory regret for having killed civilians, but they came that much closer to mimicking the State's standard 'collateral damage' defence.

At the end of August the Maoists kidnapped four policemen in Bihar and demanded the release of some of their senior leaders. A few days into the hostage drama, they killed one of them, an adivasi policeman called Lucas Tete.[43] Two days later they released the other three.[44] By killing a prisoner in custody the Maoists once again harmed their own cause. It was another example of the Janus-faced morality of 'revolutionary violence' that we can expect more of in a war zone, in which tactics trump rectitude and make the world a worse place.

Not many analysts and commentators who were pained by the Maoist killing of civilians in Dantewada pointed out that at exactly the same time as the bus was blown up by the Maoists, in Kalinganagar in Orissa and in Balitutha and Potko in Jharkhand, the police had surrounded several villages and had fired on thousands of protestors resisting the takeover of their lands by the Tatas, the Jindals and Posco (the Pohang Iron and Steel Company). Even now the siege continues. The wounded cannot be taken to hospital because of the police cordons. Videos uploaded on YouTube show armed riot police massing in the hundreds, being confronted by ordinary villagers, some of whom are armed with bows and arrows.

The one favour Operation Green Hunt has done ordinary people is that it has clarified things to them. Even the children in the villages know that the police works for the 'companies' and that Operation Green Hunt isn't a war against Maoists. It's a war against the poor.

There's nothing small about what's going on. We are watching a democracy turning on itself, trying to eat its own limbs. We're watching incredulously as those limbs refuse to be eaten.

~

Of all the various political formations involved in the current insurrection, none is more controversial than the CPI (Maoist). The most obvious reason is its unapologetic foregrounding of armed struggle as the only path to revolution. Sumanta Banerjee's book *In the Wake of Naxalbari* is one of the most comprehensive accounts of the movement.[45] It documents the early years, the almost harebrained manner in which the Naxalites tried to jump-start the Indian Revolution by 'annihilating the class enemy' and expecting the masses to rise up spontaneously. It describes the contortions it had to make in order to remain aligned with China's foreign policy, how it spread from state to state and how Naxalism was mercilessly crushed.

Buried deep inside the fury that is directed against the CPI (Maoist) by the orthodox Left, and the liberal intelligentsia, is their unease with themselves, and a puzzling, almost mystical protectiveness towards the Indian State. It's as though, when they are faced with a situation that has genuine revolutionary potential, they blink. They find reasons to look away. Political parties and individuals who have not in the last twenty-five years ever lent their support to, say, the Narmada Bachao Andolan or marched in solidarity with any one of the many peaceful people's movements in the country, have suddenly begun to extol the virtues of non-violence and Gandhian satyagraha. On the other hand, those who have been actively involved in these struggles may strongly disagree with the Maoists—they may be wary, even exasperated by them—but they *do* see them as a part of the same resistance.

It's hard to say who dislikes the Maoists more—the Indian State, its army of strategic experts and its instinctively right-wing middle class, or the Communist Party of India (CPI) and the Communist Party of India (Marxist), usually called the CPM, the several splinter groups that were part of the original Marxist-Leninists or the liberal Left. The argument begins with nomenclature. The more orthodox Communists do not believe that 'Maoism' is an 'ism' at all. The Maoists in turn call the mainstream Communist parties 'social fascists' and accuse them of 'economism'—basically, of gradually bargaining away the prospect of revolution.

Each faction believes itself to be the only genuinely revolutionary Marxist party or political formation. Each believes the other has misinterpreted Communist theory and misunderstood history. Anyone who isn't a card-carrying member of one or the other group will be able to see that none of them is entirely wrong or entirely right about what they say. But bitter splits, not unlike those in religious sects, are the natural corollary of the rigid conformity to the party line demanded by all Communist parties. So they dip into a pool of insults that dates back to the Russian and Chinese revolutions, to the great debates between Lenin, Trotsky and Stalin, to Chairman Mao's red book, and hurl them at each other. They accuse each other of the 'incorrect application' of 'Marxist-Leninist-Mao Zedong Thought', almost as though it's an ointment that's being rubbed in the wrong place. (My earlier essay 'Walking with the Comrades' landed directly in the flight path of this debate. It received its fair share of entertaining insults, which deserve a pamphlet of their own.)

Other than the debate about whether or not to enter electoral politics, the major disagreement between the various strands of Communism in India centres on their reading of whether conditions in the country are ripe for revolution. Is the prairie ready for the fire, as Mao announced in China, or is it still too damp for the single spark to ignite it? The trouble is that India lives in several centuries simultaneously, so perhaps the prairie, that vast stretch of flat grassland, is the wrong analogy for India's social and political landscape. Maybe a warren would be a better one. To arrive at a consensus about the timing of the revolution is probably impossible. So everybody marches to their own drumbeat. The CPI and the CPM have more or less postponed the revolution to the afterlife. For Charu Mazumdar, founder of the

Naxalite movement, it was meant to have happened thirty years ago. According to Ganapathy, current chief of the Maoists, it's about fifty years away.

Today, forty years after the Naxalbari uprising, the main charge against the Maoists by the parliamentary Left continues to be what it always has been. They are accused of suffering from what Lenin called an 'infantile disorder', of substituting mass politics with militarism and of not having worked at building a genuinely revolutionary proletariat. They are seen as having contempt for the urban working class, of being an ideologically ossified force that can only function as a frog-on-the-back of 'innocent' (read 'primitive') jungle-dwelling tribal people who, according to orthodox Marxists, have no real revolutionary potential. (This is not the place, perhaps, to debate a vision that says people have to first become wage-earners, enslaved to a centralized industrial system, before they can be considered revolutionary.)

The charge that the Maoists are irrelevant to urban working-class movements, to the Dalit movement, to the plight of farmers and agricultural workers outside the forests is true. There is no doubt that the Maoist party's militarized politics makes it almost impossible for it to function in places where there is no forest cover. However, it could equally be argued that the major Communist parties have managed to survive in the mainstream only by compromising their ideologies so drastically that it is impossible to tell the difference between them and other bourgeois political parties any more. It could be argued that the smaller factions that have remained relatively uncompromised have managed to do so because they do not pose a threat to anybody.

Whatever their faults or achievements as bourgeois parties, few would associate the word 'revolutionary' with the CPI or the CPM any more. (The CPI is involved in a struggle against the Posco plant in Orissa. But it is only demanding that the plant be relocated.) Even in their chosen sphere of influence, they cannot claim to have done a great service to the proletariat they say they represent. Apart from their traditional bastions in Kerala and West Bengal, both of which they are losing their grip over, they have very little presence in any other part of the country, urban or rural, forest or plains. They have run their trade unions into the ground. They have not been able to stanch the massive job losses and the virtual disbanding of the formal workforce that mechanization and the new economic policies have caused. They have not been able to prevent the systematic dismantling of workers' rights. They have managed to alienate themselves almost completely from adivasi and Dalit communities. In Kerala, many would say that they have done a better job than other political parties, but their thirty-year 'rule' in West Bengal has left that state in ruins. The repression they unleashed in Nandigram and Singur, and now against the adivasis of Jangalmahal, will probably drive them out of power for a few years. (Only for as long as it takes Mamata Banerjee of the Trinamool Congress to prove that she is not the vessel into which people should pour their hopes.) Still, while listing a litany of their sins, it must be said that the demise of the mainstream Communist parties is not something to be celebrated. At least not unless it makes way for a new, more vital and genuinely Left movement in India.

The Maoists (in their current as well as earlier avatars) have had a different political trajectory. The redistribution of land, by violent means if necessary, was always the centrepiece of their political activity. They have been completely unsuccessful in that endeavour. But their militant interventions, in which thousands of their cadre—as well as ordinary people—paid with their lives, shone a light on the deeply embedded structural injustice of Indian society. If nothing else, from the time of the Telangana movement, which, in some ways was a precursor to the uprising in Naxalbari, the Naxalite movement, for all its faults, sparked an anger about being exploited, and a desire for self-respect in some of India's most oppressed communities. In West Bengal, it led to Operation Barga (sharecropper) and, to a far lesser extent, it shamed the government in Andhra Pradesh into carrying out some land reform. Even today, all the talk about 'uneven development' and 'exploitation' of tribal areas by the prime minister, the government's plans to transfer joint forest management funds from the Forest Department directly to the gram panchayats, the Planning Commission's announcement that it will allocate ₹140 billion for tribal development, has not come from genuine concern: it has come as a strategy to defuse the Maoist 'menace'.[46] If those funds do end up benefiting the adivasi community, instead of being siphoned away by middlemen, then the 'menace' surely ought to be given some credit. Interestingly, though the Maoists have virtually no political presence outside forested areas, they do have a presence in the popular imagination, an increasingly sympathetic one, as a party that stands up for the poor against the intimidation and bullying of the State. If Operation Green Hunt becomes an outright war instead of a 'sub-conventional' one, if ordinary adivasis start dying in huge numbers, that sympathy could ignite in unexpected ways.

Among the most serious charges levelled against the Maoists is that its leaders have a vested interest in keeping people poor and illiterate in order to retain their hold on them. Critics ask why, after working in areas like Dandakaranya for thirty years, they still do not run schools and clinics, why they don't have check dams and advanced agriculture, and why people were still dying of malaria and malnutrition. Good question. But it ignores the reality of what it means to be a banned organization whose members—even if they are doctors or teachers— are liable to be shot on sight. It would be more useful to direct the same question to the Government of India that has none of these constraints. Why is it that in tribal areas that are not overrun by Maoists there are no schools, no hospitals, no check dams? Why do people in Chhattisgarh suffer from such acute malnutrition that doctors have begun to call it 'nutritional AIDS' because of the effect it has on the human immune system?

In their censored chapter in the Ministry of Panchayati Raj report, Ajay Dandekar and Chitrangada Choudhury (no fans of the Maoists—they call the party ideology 'brutal and cynical') write:

> So the Maoists today have a dual effect on the ground in PESA areas. By virtue of the gun they wield, they are able to evoke some fear in the administration at the village/block/district level. They consequently prevent the common villager's powerlessness over the neglect or violation of protective laws like PESA e.g. warning a *talathi*, who might be demanding bribes in return for

fulfilling the duty mandated to him under the Forest Rights Act, a trader who might be paying an exploitative rate for forest produce, or a contractor who is violating the minimum wage. The party has also done an immense amount of rural development work, such as mobilizing community labour for farm ponds, rainwater harvesting and land conservation works in the Dandakaranya region, which villagers testified, had improved their crops and improved their food security situation.

In their recently published empirical analysis of the working of the National Rural Employment Guarantee Scheme (NREGA) in 200 Maoist-affected districts in Orissa, Chhattisgarh and Jharkhand, which appeared in the *Economic and Political Weekly*, the authors Kaustav Banerjee and Partha Saha say:

> The field survey revealed that the charge that the Maoists have been blocking developmental schemes does not seem to hold much ground. In fact, Bastar seems to be doing much better in terms of NREGA than some other areas.... On top of that, the enforcement of minimum wages can be traced back to the wage struggles led by the Maoists in that area. A clear result that we

ADIVASI WAGE LABOURERS AT AN ALUMINIUM REFINERY, ORISSA

Now that mining companies have polluted rivers, mined away state boundaries, wrecked ecosystems and unleashed civil war, the consequences are playing out like an ancient lament over ruined landscapes and the bodies of the poor.

INDUSTRIAL DEBRIS, KEONJHAR, ORISSA

The first step towards reimagining a world gone
terribly wrong would be to stop the annihilation
of those who have a different imagination—an
imagination that is outside of capitalism as
well as Communism. An imagination which
has an altogether different understanding of
what constitutes happiness and fulfilment. To
gain this philosophical space, it is necessary to
concede some physical space for the survival
of those who may look like the keepers of our
past but who may really be the guides to our
future. To do this, we have to ask our rulers:
Can you leave the water in the rivers, the trees
in the forest? Can you leave the bauxite in
the mountain?

came across is the doubling of wage rates for tendu leaf collection in most of the Maoist areas....Also, the Maoists have been encouraging the conduct of social audits since this helps in the creation of a new kind of democratic practice hitherto unseen in India.[47]

Implicit in a lot of the debate around Maoists is the old, patronizing tendency to cast 'the masses', the adivasi people in this case, in the role of the dimwitted horde, completely controlled by a handful of wicked 'outsiders'. One university professor, a well-known Maoist-baiter, accused the leaders of the party of being parasites preying on poor adivasis.[48] To bolster his case he compared the lack of development in Dandakaranya to the prosperity in Kerala. After suggesting that the non-adivasi leaders were all cowards 'hiding safely in the forest', he appealed to all adivasi Maoist guerrillas and village militia to surrender before a panel of middle-class Gandhian activists (hand-picked by him). He called for the non-adivasi leadership to be tried for war crimes. Why non-adivasi Gandhians are acceptable, but not non-adivasi Maoists, he did not say. There is something very disturbing about this inability to credit ordinary people with being capable of weighing the odds and making their own decisions.

In Orissa, for instance, there are a number of diverse

struggles being waged by unarmed resistance movements that often have sharp differences with each other. And yet, between them all, they have managed to temporarily stop some major corporations from being able to proceed with their projects—the Tatas in Kalinganagar, Posco in Jagatsinghpur, Vedanta in Niyamgiri. Unlike in Bastar, where they control territory and are well-entrenched, the Maoists tend to use Orissa only as a corridor for their squads to pass through. But as the security forces close in on peaceful movements and ratchet up the repression, local people have to think very seriously about the pros and cons of involving the Maoist party in their struggles. Will its armed squads stay and fight the State repression that will inevitably follow a Maoist 'action'? Or will they retreat and leave unarmed people to deal with police terror? Activists and ordinary people falsely accused of being Maoists are already being jailed. Many have been killed in cold blood. But a tense, uneasy dance continues between the unarmed resistance and the CPI (Maoist). On occasion the party has done irresponsible things that have led to horrible consequences for ordinary people. In 2008, in Kandhamal district, the Maoists shot dead Laxmanananda Saraswati, leader of the Vishwa Hindu Parishad, a fascist outfit of proselytizers working among adivasis to bring them 'back into the Hindu fold'.[49] After the murder, enraged Kandha tribals who had been recently 'returned' to Hinduism were encouraged to go on a rampage. Almost 400 villages were convulsed with anti-Christian violence. Many Christians, adivasis as well as Dalits were killed, more than 200 churches burnt; tens of thousands had to flee their homes. Two years later, many of them are still not able to return to their homes. Thousands of people are spiralling into destitution, migrating to nearby towns in search of a means of survival, making the women folk, as always, the most vulnerable. The Hindu fascists have tightened their grip on the area. They are doing their best to mine the adivasi–Dalit divide and to force conversions from Christianity back to Hinduism. In Narayanpatna in Koraput district on the other hand, the situation is somewhat different. The Chasi Mulia Adivasi Sangh, which the police say is a Maoist 'front', is fighting to restore to adivasis land that was illegally appropriated by local moneylenders and liquor dealers. There have been serious internecine battles among the various political groups and the area is reeling under police terror, with hundreds of adivasis thrown into Koraput jail and thousands living in the forests. In June 2009 the Maoists killed ten Orissa state police in a landmine blast. It gave the state government an excuse to deploy the CRPF in villages and begin combing operations. And yet, from several accounts, the movement is becoming more and more militant, with thousands of adivasis rallying, coming together to cultivate land they have reclaimed right under the security force's nose. It's an old story in India—without militant resistance the poor get pulverized. The minute the resistance becomes effective, the State moves in with all the armed might at its disposal.

People who live in situations like this do not have easy choices. They certainly do not simply take instructions from a handful of ideologues who appear out of nowhere waving guns. Their decisions on what strategies to employ take into account a whole host of considerations: the history of the struggle, the nature of the repression, the urgency of the situation and, quite crucially, the landscape in which their struggle is taking place. The decision whether to be a Gandhian or a Maoist, militant or peaceful, or a bit of both (like in Nandigram) is not always a moral or ideological one. Quite often it's a tactical one. Gandhian satyagraha, for example, is a kind of political theatre. In order for it to be effective, it needs a sympathetic audience, which villagers deep in the forest do not have. When a posse of 800 policemen lay a cordon around a forest village at night and begin to burn houses and shoot people, will a hunger strike help? (Can starving people go on a hunger strike? And do hunger strikes work when they're not on TV?) Equally, guerrilla warfare is a strategy that villages in the plains, with no cover for tactical retreat, cannot afford. Sometimes, tactics get confused with ideology and lead to unnecessary internecine battles. Fortunately ordinary people are capable of breaking through ideological categories, and of being Gandhian in Jantar Mantar, militant in the plains and guerrilla fighters in the forest without necessarily suffering from a crisis of identity. The strength of the insurrection in India is its diversity, not uniformity.

Since the government has expanded its definition of 'Maoist' to include anybody who opposes it, it shouldn't come as a surprise that the Maoists have moved to centre stage. However, their doctrinal inflexibility, their reputed inability to countenance dissent, or work with other political formations, and most of all their single-minded, grim, military imagination make them too small to fill the giant pair of boots that is currently on offer.

(When I met Comrade Roopi in the forest, the first thing the tech-whiz did after greeting me was to ask about an interview I did soon after the Maoists had attacked Rani Bodili, a girls' school in Dantewada that had been turned into a police camp.[50] More than fifty policemen and SPOs were killed in the attack.[51] 'We were glad that you refused to condemn our Rani Bodili attack, but then in the same interview you said that if the Maoists ever come to power the first person we would hang would probably be you. Why did you say that? Why do you think we're like that?' I was settling into my long answer, but we were distracted. I would probably have started with Stalin's purges—in which millions of ordinary people and almost half of the 75,000 Red Army officers were either jailed or shot, and 98 out of 139 Central Committee members were arrested; gone on to the huge price people paid for China's Great Leap Forward and the Cultural Revolution; and might have ended with the Pedamallapuram incident in Andhra Pradesh, when the Maoists, in their previous avatar of People's War Group, killed the village sarpanch and assaulted women activists for refusing to obey their call to boycott elections.)

Coming back to the question: who can fill this giant pair of boots? Perhaps it cannot, and should not, be a single pair of feet. Sometimes it seems very much as though those who have a radical vision for a newer, better world do not have the steel it takes to resist the military onslaught, and those who have the steel do not have the vision.

Right now the Maoists are the most militant end of a bandwidth of resistance movements fighting an assault on adivasi homelands by a cartel of mining and infrastructure companies. To deduce from this that the CPI (Maoist) is a party with a new way of thinking about 'development' or the environment might be a little far-fetched. (The one reassuring sign is that it has cautiously said that it is against big dams. If it means what it says, that alone would automatically lead to a radically different development model.) For a political party that is widely seen as opposing the onslaught of corporate mining, the Maoists' policy (and practice) on mining remains pretty woolly. In several places where people are fighting mining companies, there is a persistent view that the Maoists are not averse to allowing mining and mining-related infrastructure projects to go ahead as long as they are given protection money. From interviews and statements made by their senior leaders on the subject of mining, what emerges is a sort of 'we'll do a better job' approach. They vaguely promise 'environmentally sustainable' mining, higher royalties, better resettlement for the displaced and higher stakes for the 'stakeholders'. (The present Indian mining minister, thinking along the same lines, recently promised that 26 per cent of the profits from mining would go to local tribals displaced by mines. What a feast *that* will be for the pigs at the trough!)

But let's take a brief look at the star attraction in the mining belt—the several trillion dollars' worth of bauxite. There *is* no environmentally sustainable way of mining bauxite and processing it into aluminium. It's a highly toxic process that most Western countries have exported out of their own environments. To produce one tonne of aluminium, you need about six tonnes of bauxite, more than a thousand tonnes of water and a massive amount of electricity.[51] For that amount of captive water and electricity, you need big dams, which, as we know, come with their own cycle of cataclysmic destruction. Last of all—the big question—what is the aluminium for? Where is it going? Aluminium is a principal ingredient in the weapons industry—for other countries' weapons industries. Given this, what would a sane, 'sustainable' mining policy be? Suppose, for the sake of argument, the CPI (Maoist) were given control of the so-called Red Corridor, the tribal homeland—with its riches of uranium, bauxite, limestone, dolomite, coal, tin, granite, marble—how would it go about the business of policy making and governance? Would it mine minerals to put on the market in order to create revenue, build infrastructure and expand its operations? Or would it mine only enough to meet people's basic needs? How would it define 'basic needs'? For instance, would nuclear weapons be a 'basic need' in a Maoist nation state?

Judging from what is happening in Russia and China and even Vietnam, eventually Communist and capitalist societies seem to have one thing in common—the DNA of their dreams. After their revolutions, after building societies that millions of workers and peasants paid for with their lives, these countries now have begun to reverse some of the gains of their revolutions and have turned into unbridled capitalist economies. For them, too, the ability to consume has become the yardstick by which progress is measured. For this kind of 'progress', you need industry. To feed the industry, you need a steady supply of raw material. For that you need mines, dams, domination, colonies, war. Old powers are waning, new ones rising. Same story, different characters—rich countries plundering poor ones. Yesterday it was Europe and the United States, today it's India and China. Maybe tomorrow it will be Africa. Will there be a tomorrow? Perhaps it's too late to ask, but then hope has little to do with reason.

Can we expect that an alternative to what looks like certain death for the planet will come from the imagination that has brought about this crisis in the first place? It seems unlikely. The alternative, if there is one, will emerge from the places and the people who have resisted the hegemonic impulse of capitalism and imperialism instead of being co-opted by it.

Here in India, even in the midst of all the violence and greed, there is still hope. If anyone can do it, we can. We still have a population that has not yet been completely colonized by that consumerist dream. We have a living tradition of those who have struggled for

Gandhi's vision of sustainability and self-reliance, for socialist ideas of egalitarianism and social justice. We have Ambedkar's vision, which challenges the Gandhians as well as the socialists in serious ways. We have the most spectacular coalition of resistance movements, with their experience, understanding and vision.

Most important of all, India has a surviving adivasi population of almost 100 million. They are the ones who still know the secrets of sustainable living. If they disappear, they will take those secrets with them. Wars like Operation Green Hunt will make them disappear. So victory for the prosecutors of these wars will contain within itself the seeds of destruction, not just for adivasis but, eventually, for the human race. That's why the war in central India is so important. That's why we need a real and urgent conversation between all those political formations that are resisting this war.

The day capitalism is forced to tolerate non-capitalist societies in its midst and to acknowledge limits in its quest for domination, the day it is forced to recognize that its supply of raw material will not be endless, is the day when change will come. If there is any hope for the world at all, it does not live in climate-change conference rooms or in cities with tall buildings. It lives low down on the ground, with its arms around the people who go to battle every day to protect their forests, their mountains and their rivers because they know that the forests, the mountains and the rivers protect them.

The first step towards reimagining a world gone terribly wrong would be to stop the annihilation of those who have a different imagination—an imagination that is outside of capitalism as well as Communism. An imagination which has an altogether different understanding of what constitutes happiness and fulfilment. To gain this philosophical space, it is necessary to concede some physical space for the survival of those who may look like the keepers of our past but who may really be the guides to our future. To do this, we have to ask our rulers: Can you leave the water in the rivers, the trees in the forest? Can you leave the bauxite in the mountain? If they say they cannot, then perhaps they should stop preaching morality to the victims of their wars.

September 2010

NOTES

MR CHIDAMBARAM'S WAR

1. 'The World's Billionaires: #230 Anil Agarwal', Forbes.com, 8 March 2007; Peter Popham, 'Indian Villagers Pay a High Price as Commodity Boom Comes to Rural Orissa', *Independent* (London), 4 August 2006; 'The Vedanta Affair: The Nub of the CEC's Report Is the Issue of Forest Land', *Telegraph* (India), 27 November 2005, www.telegraphindia.com/1051127/asp/opinion/story_5528395.asp.

2. Press Trust of India, 'Naxalism Biggest Internal Security Challenge: PM', 13 April 2006, www.hindustantimes.com/Naxalism-biggest-challenge -PM/Article1-86531.aspx.

3. Manmohan Singh, 'Full Text of Manmohan Singh's Speech at CMs Meet', IBN Live, 6 January 2009, http://ibnlive.in.com/news/full-text-of -manmohan-singhs-speech-at-cms-meet/82035-3.html.

4. Jawed Naqvi, 'Singh Sees "Vital Interest" in Peace with Pakistan', *Dawn*, 9 June 2009, www.dawn.com/wps/wcm/connect/dawn-content-library/ dawn/news/world/04-india-pm-willing-meet-pakistan-qs-08; http:// pmindia.nic.in/speeches.htm

5. Rahul Pandita, 'We Shall Certainly Defeat the Government', *Open*, 17 October 2009, www.openthemagazine.com/article/nation/ we-shall-certainly-defeat-the-government.

6. *Development Challenges in Extremist Affected Areas*, Report of an Expert Group to Planning Commission (New Delhi: Government of India, 2008), 59–60.

7. Saikat Datta, 'On War Footing', *Outlook*, 13 October 2009. See also Chhattisgarh Visthapan Virodhi Manch (Chhattisgarh Anti-Displacement Platform), leaflet, Raipur, India, 6 October 2009, http://radicalnotes.com/ journal/2009/10/30/raipur-rally-against-displacement-oct-6-2009/.

8. 'India, Pak Unite to Block Anti-Lanka Move at UN', IndianExpress.com, 29 May 2009, www.indianexpress.com/news/india-pak-unite-to-block -antilanka-move-at/467703/.

9. On 24 December 2010 a sessions court in Raipur held Dr Binayak Sen guilty of sedition and sentenced him to life imprisonment.

10. Justice P.B. Sawant, remarks at hearing of Citizens Initiative for Peace, Speakers Hall, Constitution Club, New Delhi, 20 October 2009.

11. Hargopal, remarks at hearing of Citizens Initiative for Peace, Speakers Hall, Constitution Club, New Delhi, 20 October 2009.

12. Project Report by ITM EEC, Batch 20, Group 6, Pankal Tiwary, et al., *Where Is the Land Going? A Study on Land Grabbing with Reference to Reliance Maha Munabi SEZ* (2009), www.scribd.com/doc/26213514/ Batch20-Group-6-Macro-Economics-Project-Report.

13. Samarendra Das and Felix Padel, *Out of This Earth: East India Adivasis and the Aluminium Cartel* (New Delhi: Orient BlackSwan, 2010); United Nations Human Development Report 2009, http://hdrstats.undp.org/ en/indicators/150.html.

14. P. Sainath, 'Mass Media: Masses of Money?' *India Together*, 25 December 2009, www.indiatogether.org/2009/dec/psa-masses.htm.

15. Paranjoy Guha Thakurta, 'Fix-Ed Case', *Tehelka*, 14 November 2009, www.tehelka.com/story_main43.asp?filename=Bu141109fixed_case.asp; 'Chidambaram Faces Flak on Vedanta Links', *Business Standard*, 9 August 2006, www.business-standard.com/india/news/chidambaram-faces -flakvedanta-links/257339/.

16. Manoj Mitta, 'Petitioners Didn't Have Say on Kapadia Presence', *Times of India*, 13 October 2009.

17. Man Mohan, 'College That Trains Cops to Take on Naxalites', Tribune Online (Chandigarh, India), 20 July 2009, www.tribuneindia.com/2009/ 20090720/main8.htm.

18. Ashok Mitra, 'The Phantom Enemy', *Telegraph* (India), 23 October 2009.

WALKING WITH THE COMRADES

1. Trevor Selvam, 'India for Selective Assassination of Its Own Citizens?' Countercurrents.org, 31 January 2010, www.countercurrents.org/ selvam310110.htm.

2. Canary Trap, 'Karnataka Lok Ayukta Report on Illegal Mining', 21 January 2010, http://canarytrap.in/2010/01/21/karnataka -lokayukta-report-on-illegal-mining/.

3. Man Mohan, 'College That Trains Cops to Take on Naxalites', Tribune Online (Chandigarh, India), 20 July 2009, www.tribuneindia .com/2009/20090720/main8.htm.

4. Shoma Chaudhury, 'The Quiet Soldiers of Compassion', *Tehelka*, 23 August 2008.

5. Press Trust of India, 'Naxalism Biggest Internal Security Challenge: PM', 13 April 2006, www.hindustantimes.com/Naxalism-biggest-challenge -PM/Article1-86531.aspx.

6. See the Ministry of Rural Development's draft report of the Committee on State Agrarian Relations and the Unfinished Task of Land Reform, Vol. 1 (March 2009), www.rd.ap.gov.in/IKPLand/MRD_Committee

_Report_V_01_Mar_09.pdf, and compare this with the final report, http://dolr.nic.in/Committee%20Report.doc.

7. See *Frontline*, 21 October 2005.

8. The Human Rights Forum (HRF) denies that Balagopal made such a press release.

9. See Judgement of the Supreme Court of India on Mohammad Afzal vs the State (NCT of Delhi), 4 August 2005.

10. Charu Mazumdar, 'Hate, Stamp and Smash Centrism', May 1970, in *The Collected Works of Charu Mazumdar* (Deshabrati Prakashani, publishing house of the Undivided C.P.I. [M-L]), transcribed on the Marxist Internet Archive, www.marxists.org/reference/archive/mazumdar/1970/05/x01.htm.

TRICKLEDOWN REVOLUTION

1. Anonymous, 'The Goose and the Commons', *Tickler*, 1 February 1821.

2. Address by Prime Minister Manmohan Singh, Oxford University, Oxford, United Kingdom, 8 July 2005.

3. Samanth Subramanian and Krish Raghav, 'The Economics of the Games', *Wall Street Journal* and LiveMint.com, 26 October 2010, www.livemint.com/2009/10/26205604/The-economics-of-the-Games.html.

4. See Geeta Pandey, 'Delhi Street Vendors Evicted before Commonwealth Games', BBC News, Delhi, 20 August 2010.

5. 'Delhi to Banish Beggars Ahead of Commonwealth Games', *Times of India*, 1 September 2009.

6. 'Nearly 80% of India Lives on Half Dollar a Day', Reuters, 8 August 2007, www.reuters.com/article/idUSDEL218894; 'Foodgrains That Could Feed 1.4 Crore People Rot', CNN-IBN, 27 July 2010.

7. Central Statistical Organization, Ministry of Statistics and Programme Implementation, Government of India, *Millennium Development Goals—India Country Report 2009*. See also United Nations, *The Millennium Development Goals Report 2009* (New York: United Nations, 2009), p. 12.

8. Emily Wax and Rama Lakshmi, 'As Commonwealth Games Loom, "Unfit" Athletes' Village Adds to India's Problems', *Washington Post*, 24 September 2010.

9. Jason Burke, 'More of World's Poor Live in India Than in All Sub-Saharan Africa, Says Study', *The Guardian* (London), 14 July 2010.

10. Prime Minsiter Manmohan Singh, Indian Independence Day Speech, Red Fort, New Delhi, 15 August 2010.

11. C.P. Chandrasekhar, 'How Significant Is IT in India?' *The Hindu*, 31 May 2010.

12. 'India Needs Labour Transitions to Remove Poverty', Reuters, 6 April 2009.

13. S. Sakthivel and Pinaki Joddar, 'Unorganised Sector Workforce in India: Trends, Patterns and Social Security Coverage', *Economic and Political Weekly*, 27 May 2006.

14. Utsa Patnaik, 'Food Stocks and Hunger in India', paper, 3 August 2002, www.macroscan.org/pol/aug02/pol030802Food_Stocks.htm.

15. 'Mukesh Ambani Tops for the Third Year as India's Richest', *Forbes Asia*, 30 September 2010. The article notes: The combined net worth of India's 100 richest people is $300 billion, up from $276 billion last year. This year, there are 69 billionaires on the India Rich List, 17 more than last year.' India's 2009 GDP was $1.2 trillion.

16. The Associated Press reported in October 2010, 'Today, in a country where 300 million people live on less than $1 a day, the economy is growing at nearly 9 percent and the rich shop for Porsches and Louis Vuitton purses. The number of Indian millionaires jumped by 51 percent last year, reaching more than 127,000.' Tim Sullivan, 'Indian Cram School Town Redraws Lines of Success', Associated Press, 24 October 2010.

17. Ashok Mitra, *A Prattler's Tale: Bengal, Marxism, Governance*, translated from the Bengali by Sipra Bhattacharya (Kolkata: Samya Books, 2007).

18. 'I Am Your Soldier in Delhi: Rahul to Tribals', Press Trust of India, 26 August 2010.

19. P. Chidambaram, The Harish C. Mahindra 2007 Lecture, 'Poor Rich Countries: The Challenges of Development', Harvard University South Asia Initiative, Cambridge, Massachusetts, 18 October 2007; www.indianembassy.org/prdetail697/finance-minister-mr.-p.-chidambaram's-speech-at-the-harvard-university-south-asia-initiative-the-harish-c.-mahindra-2007-lecture-on-andquot%3Bpoor-rich-countries%3A-the-challenges-of-developmentandquot%3B.

20. Ajay Dandekar and Chitrangada Choudhury, 'PESA, Left Wing Extremism and Governance: Concerns and Challenges in India's Tribal Districts', Institute of Rural Management, Anand, commissioned by Ministry of Panchayati Raj, Government of India, New Delhi, no date, www.tehelka.com/channels/News/2010/july/10/PESAchapter.pdf.

21. Raman Kirpal, 'Why You Must Read This Censored Chapter', *Tehelka*, 10 July 2010.

22. Ernesto Guevara, *Guerrilla Warfare,* third ed., eds. Brian Loveman and Thomas M. Davies, Jr (Rowman and Littlfield, 2002), p. 51.

23. Jawed Naqvi, 'Singh Sees "Vital Interest" in Peace with Pakistan', *Dawn*, 9 June 2009; http://pmindia.nic.in/speeches.htm

Notes

24. Bhagat Singh's Last Petition, no date, www.shahidbhagatsingh.org/index.asp?link=bhagat_petition.

25. B.G.Verghese, 'Daylight at the Thousand-Star Hotel', *Outlook*, 3 May 2010.

26. Chemkuri [Cherukuri] Azad Rajkumar, 'A Last Note to a Neo-Colonialist', *Outlook*, 19 July 2010.

27. Partho Sarathi Ray, 'The Rs. 1500 Crore "Maoist Empire" or How the Police Plants Stories in the Press', *Sanhati*, 16 April 2010.

28. 'Chhattisgarh on Top Alert after Deadly Naxal Attack', Press Trust of India, 18 May 2010; Joseph John, 'Maoists Chopped Limbs, Slit Throats of Injured CRPF Men', www.indianexpress.com/news/maoists-chopped-limbs-slit-throats-of-injur/641291/

29. Rakhi Chakrabarty, 'Raped Repeatedly, Naxal Leader Quits Red Ranks', *Times of India*, 24 August 2010.

30. 'Air Chief Releases Joint Doctrines', Ministry of Defence, 16 June 2010. See also 'Armed Forces Release New Warfare Doctrine', Press Trust of India, 16 June 2010; and 'Armed Forces Release Two Doctrines on Joint Warfare', Press Trust of India, 16 June 2010.

31. Gautam Navlakha, 'Azad's Assassination: An Insight into the Indian State's Response to Peoples' Resistance', *Sanhati*, 25 July 2010.

32. 'Get Ready to Fight Naxals, Said Chief. Or Did He?' *Indian Express*, 17 July 2010. The article notes, interestingly, 'Hours after it put out a press release . . . the Defence wing of the Press Information Bureau withdrew the release. No reason was assigned.'

33. 'IAF Can Fire in Self-Defence during Anti-Maoist Operations', *Hindustan Times*, 12 August 2010.

34. See Justice (Retired) B.P. Jeevan Reddy, *Report of the Committee to Review the Armed Forces (Special Powers) Act 1958*, submitted to the Government of India in June 2005.

35. Supriya Sharma, 'Finally, Army Moves into Maoist Territory', *Times of India*, 14 December 2010.

36. 'Edited Text of 12,262-word Response by Azad, Spokesperson, Central Committee, CPI (Maoist)', *The Hindu*, 14 April 2010.

37. South Asia Terrorism Portal, Table: 'Fatalities in Left-wing Extremism—2010', www.satp.org/satporgtp/countries/india/maoist/data_sheets/fatalitiesnaxal.asp.

38. 'Wanted Naxals Protected by Forests, Mines', Indo-Asian News Service, Raipur, 8 April 2010.

39. Azad, 'Hail the Daring and the Biggest Ever Guerrilla Attack on the Hired Mercenaries of the Indian State Carried Out by the Heroic PLGA Guerrillas in Chhattisgarh!' press statement for the Central Committee of the CPI (Maoist), 8 April 2010.

40. 'Fresh Maoist Attacks Feared in Chhattisgarh Towns', Sify News, 9 April 2010.

41. Ashish Khetan, 'CRPF Men Faked Log Entries to Skip Patrolling', *India Today*, 19 May 2010. Also see E.N. Rammohan Committee report.

42. '44 Killed as Maoists Blow Up Bus in Dantewada', *Times of India*, 18 May 2010.

43. 'Bihar Abduction: Body of Havildar Lucas Recovered', *Indian Express*, 3 September 2010.

44. 'Bihar Hostage Crisis Over, Maoists Release 3 Abducted Cops', *Times of India*, 6 September 2010.

45. Sumanta Banerjee, *In the Wake of Naxalbari: A History of the Naxalite Movement in India* (Calcutta: Subarnarekha, 1980).

46. 'Rs 14000cr Maoist Balm', *Telegraph* (Calcutta), 6 July 2010.

47. Kaustav Banerjee and Partha Saha, 'The NREGA, the Maoists and the Developmental Woes of the Indian State', *Economic and Political Weekly*, 10 July 2010.

48. Nirmalangshu Mukherji, 'Arms Over People', *Outlook*, 19 May 2010.

49. Quoting the 'Aims and Objects of Vishva Hindu Parishad', no date.

50. See Arundhati Roy, *The Shape of the Beast: Conversations with Arundhati Roy* (New Delhi: Viking, Penguin India, 2008), pp. 225–30.

51. Press Trust of India, 'Chhattisgarh: 55 Killed in Naxal Bloodbath', 15 March 2007.

52. Samarendra Das and Felix Padel, *Out of This Earth: East India Adivasis and the Aluminium Cartel* (New Delhi: Orient BlackSwan, 2010).